Forward

People of Faith: an Interfaith Companion to the Revised Common Lectionary by John R. Mabry takes a very good thing and expands it dramatically. The three-year cycle of biblical readings created an occasion of community among Christians. A Roman Catholic could say to a Presbyterian, "Oh yes, we used those same lessons in our congregation last Sunday." Or a Lutheran could say the same to an Episcopalian. A lectionary used across ancient boundary lines of theological differences has the power to be an agent of reconciliation for a moment and perhaps a promise that something basic unifies us.

What the three-year cycle of biblical readings does for almost two billion Christians, the interfaith companion has the potential of doing for four billion believers of various faiths. We live in a world where religious people know so little that is accurate about the people of other religions. This interfaith companion provides all of us with related scriptural sources that would make it possible for people of various religions to talk over the backyard fences that separate us. Conversation. This lectionary could well be a means of encouraging a crucial conversation between Muslims and Hindus, Buddhists and Jews, and others. In a world where religious fanatics are seriously seeking weapons of mass destruction, it is essential that religious moderates find ways of talking to each other and of moving to levels of deeper understanding.

There is a moment in Christian scripture where Jesus takes Peter, James, and John to a mountaintop where he is transfigured.

"Suddenly there appeared to him Moses and Elijah talking with him" [Matthew 7:3]. We could be pedestrian and say that there was a conversation between two figures of one religion (Judaism) and the key figure of another religion (Christianity). But what was happening was of greater importance than that. At least we know that there is a conversation that goes far beyond well-defined religious borders and sensitivities. If Jesus could talk with Moses, could Jesus be in conversation with the Prophet Mohammad or the Buddha? What are the limits of transfiguration conversation? Is there a spirit of this transfiguration conversation that is released on the mountaintop, never to be extinguished? A spirit to inspire peacemakers and cause them to be blessed as well as a blessing? What are the boundaries for sacred scriptures? John Mabry gently opens doors that have always been closed and invites natural enemies to become appreciative friends.

Usually when sacred scripture is read, it is in one of two contexts. It is read with one's own group where only the people of one's own religion are talking to each other. Or it is read in public in proclamation form, hoping it will convert others to one's own religion. With the interfaith companion there is another way to read sacred scripture, i.e., in context of the sacred scripture of other traditions. Such reading will invite comparisons, point out contradictions, raise questions. In the long run I predict it will make one's own faith stand out in bolder relief while at the same time giving rise to a heightened respect for the religion of others.

Some time ago John Mabry told me that he was setting out to do this project. I wished him well, but I wondered if it could be done. Now I see it, and it sparkles. Not perfect. Nor is it the last word on the subject. But, oh my, what a gift to anyone who yearns to glimpse more of the generosity of God. Multiple groups and individuals will be enriched by this work.

The Rt. Rev. William E. Swing
Bishop of the Episcopal Diocese of California
Founder and President of the United Religions Initiative

Introduction

Many years ago I was lying in bed reading a collection of creation stories from around the world. In a moment of reverie, I remarked to my wife how much fun it would be to read these stories to the children we might someday have.

"I don't know," she yawned, "won't that confuse them? I mean, they won't know which one is true."

Without a moment's thought, I blurted out, "But they're all true." She cocked an eyebrow at me, but I was struck by the profundity of my offhand retort. *They are all true.*

That moment began my studies in world religions in earnest, and I eventually went on to do my doctoral studies in that subject. This led to a deep and abiding love of the scriptures of diverse traditions, to which I have returned again and again for wisdom, insight, and sheer pleasure.

The most surprising effect this has had on me is in reference to my own faith as a Christian, and my work as a minister. For every time I have journeyed out to explore a tradition other than my own, I have come home to Christianity with new treasures that have clarified, challenged, and deepened my own connection with the Divine.

This experience is not unique to me, of course. I have known (and read) many people who have reported similar fascination with the scriptures of the world's religions, and this contact has been likewise transformative for them.

The insights and knowledge I have gleaned have benefited those I am privileged to preach to and teach, as well. The congregation at our parish is delighted when a sermon opens with an explication of Hindu iconography, for example, or a story from the life of Mohammad. Many times in my ministry I have used scriptures from other traditions to augment a text under consideration from the Jewish or Christian scriptures, and the result is always satisfying and thought-provoking.

Part of the effect of working with such a variety of texts has been a rising consciousness in myself that I am not only a Christian, united through Christ with other Christians around the world and across time, I am also a Person of Faith, united through the divine Spirit that animates all beings with every other Person of Faith, of any and all traditions.

There is an old joke in which St. Peter is showing someone around heaven, and making a grand tour of all of the faith communities represented there. When he gets to the Christian section, there is a high wall around it. "Shhh," St. Peter warns the tourist, "This is where the Christians live. They think they are the only ones here."

This joke provides a funny but sad mirror for most of the Christian community, and yet, I believe many Christians are growing beyond the spiritual xenophobia that has plagued our past. The Communion of Saints, we are discovering, is much larger than we had ever imagined it. There is indeed a "Wideness in God's Mercy" of which we have hardly yet dared to dream.

More than ever before, people of different faith traditions are recognizing their common ground and common mission goals. Just as the ecumenical movement of the twentieth century saw Christians of various denominations recognizing one another as fellow members of the body of Christ, so we are witnessing a new ecumenical movement today. We are finally viewing one another as children of One Earth, and our life as springing from One Spirit.

In *People of Faith*, I hope to provide a handy resource to help foster this very sense of kinship between Christians and people of other faith traditions. For each Sunday reading of the three-year Revised Common Lectionary cycle, this book provides a "sister" reading from the scriptures of a non-Christian religion. Each selection is thematically related to the Gospel reading assigned for the day. A short summary of The Gospel reading is also provided on each page.

I have intended *People of God* to be useful in a variety of ways. Congregations open to exploring their common ground with other faith traditions may want to include these readings in liturgical proclamation. Lay people as well as clergy may want to employ the readings in their daily devotionals. Sunday school teachers and discussion group leaders can use it to begin discussions, especially where classes are lectionary-based. Ministers may also find it helpful in preparing sermons based on lectionary texts.

These readings were not chosen with a specific agenda in mind. There is no rhyme or reason to how they "illuminate" the Gospel passage they are related to. Sometimes a reading will echo and reinforce the Gospel reading—often employing spookily similar language or imagery. Sometimes, however, the readings challenge or even contradict the Gospel lesson, allowing us to sit in the midst of a conversation between two traditions. Finally, a reading may provide a twist to the Gospel reading, taking the listener or reader into an interpretive space that may not have occurred to him or her previously.

Sometimes I have designated the reading as being from the "scriptures" of a religion, and sometimes from a religion's "tradition." If I was in doubt about the canonical legitimacy of a particular reading, I have usually erred on the side of referring to it as being part of a religion's "tradition" for safety.

Some traditions are by necessity better represented than others. I have taken care, however, to make sure that no two contiguous readings are drawn from the same religious heritage.

After much consideration, I decided not to include readings

from traditions which identify as Christian yet which deviate from the Orthodox, Catholic, and Protestant interpretations of that faith (such as Mormons, Jehovah's Witnesses, and the Unification Church, among others). Partly this is out of respect for these communities' own self-identity as Christians, even though readings from these traditions would have made for some very interesting comparisons indeed. The only exceptions to this rule are the very few readings from the ancient Gnostic tradition, some of which have a Christian orientation, and some not. As there are few today who self-identify as Christian Gnostics of the Valentinian School, and since this perspective is often quite unique, I have decided to include a small number of readings from this tradition.

Finally, in choosing scriptures from the Jewish tradition, I have tried to draw mainly from extra-biblical sources. For those readings drawn from the Jewish scriptures, I have in all but two cases succeeded in avoiding texts found elsewhere in the lectionary cycle.

I am grateful to many collections of readings, including Marcus Borg's *Jesus and Buddha: The Parallel Sayings*, and Wade Hatcher's *The Complete Bhagavad Gita and the Bible: Pearls of the Same Strand*. But most especially I am indebted to Andrew Wilson's *World Scripture: A Comparative Anthology of Sacred Texts* — an invaluable resource without which this project would have been much more arduous than it has been. I am also indebted to the Rt. Rev. William Swing, founder of the United Religions Initiative, for lending a Forward to this volume.

Bishop Swing's vision of a world where religions cooperate rather than compete, and can speak with one voice on matters of peace and justice, is a constant inspiration to me, and a witness to the world. It is truly amazing what one man of vision can do, and I hope that this book, in its own small way, can contribute to this august vision. Both I and the world have come a long way since my little epiphany about the truth of the world's creation myths.

In *People of Faith* I am hoping that we may travel this road of dialogue and cooperation further, with greater intentionality, and with greater affection for one another's paths and wisdom. There is only one Earth, after all, and One Spirit who gives life to all beings. As People of Faith we have much to learn from each other, much affection to foster, much that needs our cooperation. The collective wisdom of our sacred writings is a heritage that belongs to all humankind, indeed, to all of the earth.

Year A

First Sunday of Advent

A reading from the Jain scriptures:
As the fallow leaf of the tree falls to the ground,
when its days are gone,
even so is the life of men;
Gautama, be careful all the while!

As the dew-drop dangling on the top
of a blade of grass lasts but a short time,
even so the life of men;
Gautama, be careful all the while!

A life so fleet, and existence so precarious,
wipe off all the sins you have ever committed;
Gautama, be careful all the while!

A rare chance, in the long course of time,
is human birth for a living being;
hard are the consequences of actions;
Gautama, be careful all the while!
Uttaradhyayana Sutra 10.1-4

Gospel reading for the day: Matthew 24:36-44
"You must be ready, because the Son of Man
will come at an hour when you do not expect him."

Second Sunday of Advent

A reading from the Zoroastrian scriptures:
As was the will of God, so I ought to have thought;
as was the will of God, so I ought to have spoken;
as was the will of God, so I ought to have acted.
If I have not so thought, so spoken, so acted,
then do I repent for the sin,
do I repent by my thought, word, and deed.
do I repent with all my heart and conscience.
Zend Avesta, Patet 6

Gospel reading for the day: Matthew 3:1-12
"Repent, for the kingdom of heaven has come near."

Third Sunday of Advent

A reading from the Buddhist scriptures:
The Buddha said:
Do not be satisfied with hearsay
or with tradition or with legendary lore
or with what has come down in scriptures or with conjecture
or with logical inference or with weighing evidence
or with liking for a view after pondering over it
or with someone else's ability
or with the thought, "The monk is our teacher."

When you know in yourselves:
"These things are wholesome,
blameless, commended by the wise,"
and being adopted and put into effect
they lead to welfare and happiness,
then you should practice and abide in them.
Kalama Sutta

Gospel reading for the day: Matthew 11:2-11
"Are you the one who was to come,
or should we expect someone else?"
Jesus replied, "Go back and report to John
what you hear and see: the blind receive sight,
the lame walk, those who have leprosy are cured,
the deaf hear, the dead are raised,
and the good news is preached to the poor."

Fourth Sunday of Advent

A reading from the Hindu scriptures:
When Devaki, who was like a great divinity,
was impregnated, she received seven embryos.
Kamsa killed six embryos as soon as they were born,
smashing them upon the ground.
But Sleep brought to Rohini the seventh embryo
that Devaki had received.
As if in a dream, she saw the embryo slip out of her.
Then Sleep spoke in the dark night to the terrified Rohini,
"Since this embryo was drawn out
and placed in your womb, fair lady, he will be your son,
and his name shall be Krishna."
Rehini rejoiced to receive that son,
and she lowered her face and entered the house,
shining like a constellation of stars.
Adapted from the Harivamsa

Gospel reading for the day: Matthew 1:18-25
Jesus' mother, Mary, was pledged to be married to Joseph,
but before they came together, she was found
to be with child through the Holy Spirit.

Christmas
Years ABC

A reading from the Buddhist scriptures:
When Queen Maya noticed that the time
of her delivery was approaching,
she went to a couch overspread with an awning,
thousands of waiting-women looking on
with joy in their hearts.
The propitious constellation of Pushya shone brightly
when a son was born to the queen for the healing of the world.
He came out of his mother's side,
without causing her pain or injury,
issuing from the womb as befits a Buddha.
He did not enter the world in the usual manner,
and he appeared like one descended from the sky.
His limbs shone with the radiant hue of precious gold,
and lit up the space all around.
Instantly he walked seven steps,
and spoke these words full of meaning for the future:
"For enlightenment was I born, for the good of all that lives.
This is the last time that I have been born
into this world of becoming."
Adapted from the Buddhacarita

Gospel reading for the day: Luke 2:1-14 (15-20)
While they were in Bethlehem, the time came for the baby
to be born, and Mary gave birth to her firstborn, a son.
She wrapped him in cloths and placed him in a manger,
because there was no room for them in the inn.

1st Sunday after Christmas

A reading from the Jewish tradition:
"The king of Egypt said, "When you act as midwives to the Hebrew women, if it is a boy, kill him; but if it is a girl, she shall live." But the midwives feared God; they did not do as the king of Egypt commanded them, but they let the boys live. Now a man from the house of Levi went and married a Levite woman.

The woman conceived and bore a son; and when she saw that he was a fine baby, she hid him three months. When she could hide him no longer she got a papyrus basket for him, and plastered it with bitumen and pitch; she put the child in it and placed it among the reeds on the bank of the river. The daughter of Pharaoh came down to bathe at the river, while her attendants walked beside the river. She saw the basket among the reeds and sent her maid to bring it. When she opened it, she saw the child. He was crying, and she took pity on him, "This must be one of the Hebrews' children," she said. She named him Moses, "because," she said, "I drew him out of the water."
Excerpted from Exodus 1-2

Gospel reading for the day: Matthew 2:13-23
Harod gave orders to kill all the boys in Bethlehem.
"Get up," an angel said to Joseph,
"Take the child and his mother and escape to Egypt."

Holy Name of Jesus
Years ABC

A reading from a native Middle Eastern tradition:
A rock that was hit by lighting was moving and all the broken fragments were floating around the rock. At last an outline of a human figure began to take shape. The figure was clearly human now—his face was of a young boy and then of an old bearded man, another moment, a mature man, his face was the face of all years. His head was adorned with a Phrygian cap, armed with a knife, and carrying a torch in the other hand. The assembly shouted in unison: "We have seen the birth of our Lord Mithra from the rock."

All the men dressed in the shedders clothing started moving toward Mithra, they all were carrying a sheep which they intended to offer to him. Mohran smiled and the sheep came onto his arm. He picked the sheep up and walked with the other shepherds toward Mithra. They sacrificed the sheep while saying: "We sacrifice unto Mithra, the lord of wide pastures, who is truth-speaking, a chief in assemblies, with a thousand ears, well-shapen, with ten thousand eyes, high, with full knowledge, strong, sleepless, and ever awake." Some of the older shepherds gave Lord Mithra fig leaves to cloth himself. Mithra stood up in his strength, went forth in the awfulness of royalty, and sent from his eyes beautiful looks that shone from afar.

Adapted from "The Birth of Mithra" by Payam Nabarz

Gospel reading for the day: Luke 2:15-21
When the angels had left them, the shepherds said to one another, "Let's go to Bethlehem and see this thing that has happened."

New Years
Years ABC

A reading from a native African tradition:
At the gates of the land of the dead,
you will pass before a searching Judge.
His justice is true and he will examine your feet.
He will know how to find every stain,
whether visible or hidden under the skin;
if you have fallen on the way he will know.
If the Judge finds no stains on your feet,
open your belly to joy, for you have overcome,
and your belly is clean.
Fon Song, Benin

Gospel reading for the day: Matthew 25:31-46
All the nations will be gathered before him,
and he will separate the people one from another
as a shepherd separates the sheep from the goats.

2nd Sunday after Christmas
Years ABC

A reading from the Hindu scriptures:
Whenever truth is forgotten in the world,
and wickedness prevails,
the Lord of Love becomes flesh to show the way,
the truth, and the life to humanity.
Such an incarnation is an avatar,
an embodiment of God on earth.
Srimad Bhagavatam 1.1

Gospel reading for the day: John 1:(1-9) 10-18
In the beginning was the Word,
and the Word was with God,
and the Word was God.

Epiphany
Years ABC

A reading from the Buddhist scriptures:
Now the instant the Future Buddha was conceived
in the womb of his mother, all the ten thousand worlds
suddenly quaked, quivered, and shook.
An immeasurable light spread through ten thousand worlds;
the blind recovered their sight, as if from desire to see
this his glory...the fires went out in all the hells...
celestial music was heard to play in the sky;
and the whole ten thousand worlds became one mass
of garlands of the utmost possible magnificence....
As he was issuing from his mother's womb,
he stretched out his right hand, and said,
"Tell me, mother, is there any money in the house?
I want to give alms."
After he had completely issued forth, his mother said,
"It's a wealthy family, my son, into which you are born."
And putting his hand in her own, she had them place in his a
purse containing a thousand pieces of money.
Adapted from the Introduction to the Jtaka 31, 49-51

Gospel reading for the day: Matthew 2:1-12
Magi from the east came to Jerusalem and asked,
"Where is the one who has been born king of the Jews?
We saw his star in the east and have come to worship him."

Baptism of the Lord

A reading from the Hindu scriptures:
Wash away, waters, whatever
sin is in me, what wrong I have done,
what imprecation I have uttered,
and what untruth I have spoken.
Today I have sought the waters,
we have mingled with their essence;
approach me, Agni, god of fire, with your power,
and fill me, as I am, with brilliance.
Adapted from the Rig Veda 10.9.8-9

Gospel reading for the day: Matthew 3:13-17
Jesus came to the Jordan to be baptized by John.
And a voice from heaven said, "This is my Son,
whom I love; with him I am well pleased."

Sunday between
January 14 & 20

A reading from the Buddhist scriptures:
The glowworm shines so long
as the light-bringer has not arisen.
But when the shining one has come up,
its light is quenched, it glows no longer.
Such is the shining of the sectarians.
So long as the rightly awakened ones arise not in the world,
the sophists get no light, nor do their followers,
and those of wrong views cannot be released from ill.
Udana 73

Gospel reading for the day: John 1:29-42
John the Baptist points to Jesus,
and proclaims him "the Lamb of God."

Sunday between
January 21 & 27

A reading from the Sikh scriptures:
My heart trembles, whom shall I call?
I should devote myself to the Healer of suffering,
the One who is ever and ever the Giver.
My Sovereign is always fresh,
and ever and ever the Giver.
Night and day, we must serve the Sovereign,
the One who will liberate us at last.
Hearing the Word, my sisters,
we reach the other shore.
Compassionate One, by contemplating Your Name,
we swim to the shore of liberation.
I offer myself to You a hundred times.
Dhanasri Mahalla 1

Gospel reading for the day: Matthew 4:12-23
"Come, follow me," Jesus said,
"and I will make you fishers of men."

Sunday between
January 28 & February 3

A reading from the Islamic scripture:
The servants of the All-merciful are those
who walk in the earth modestly and who,
when the ignorant address them, say, "Peace";
who pass the night prostrate to their Lord and standing;
...who, when they expend, are neither prodigal
nor parsimonious, but between that is a just stand;
and those who bear not false witness and,
when they pass by idle talk, pass by with dignity...
those shall be recompensed with the highest heaven,
for that they endured patiently, and they shall
receive therein a greeting and "peace."
Therein they shall dwell forever;
fair is it as a lodging place and an abode.
Qur'an 25:63-76

Gospel reading for the day: Matthew 5:1-12
"Blessed are the peacemakers,
for they shall be called the children of God."

Sunday between
February 4 & 10

A reading from the Jewish tradition:
When Moses reached heaven, he beheld the Lord
seated upon the Throne of Glory and occupied in adding
and ornamenting the letters of the Torah with crowns.
Moses asked him, "Why are you adding these
ornamentations to the letters?"
The Lord replied, "In the days to come there will be born
a man named Rabbi Akiba, to whom the secret of these
dots and ornamentations will be revealed."
"If it is thy will," said Moses,
"may I be permitted to behold this wise man?"
"Look behind you," said the Lord. Moses did
and beheld a house full of students being taught by a master.
The disciples asked their teacher, "How do you know this?"
and Rabbi Akiba answered, "What I have told you has
already been explained to Moses on Mt. Sinai."
When Moses heard this, he was satisfied.
But he turned to God, saying, "Lord, why did you not give
the Torah to Israel through this man instead of me?"
The Lord replied, "Such is my decree."
Talmud, Menahot 29b

Gospel reading for the day: Matthew 5:13-20
"I have not come to abolish the law and the prophets
...but to fulfill them."

Sunday between
February 11 & 17

A reading from the Jain tradition:
Disillusioned with the material world and power,
King Prasenjit renounced his kingdom and became a Jain monk.
One day while he was meditating, some of his former subjects
happened by and recognized him.
"What a fool," they said, "for he renounced his kingdom
and left his son in the care of a few wicked courtiers.
And now they are trying to kill the son and steal the throne!"
Pasenjit's blood boiled at these words,
though he remained motionless.
Outwardly, he was the very picture of calm,
though inside a fierce battle was raging.
The disciples of the Lord Mahavira praised Prasenjit's control
and asked which heaven he would go to
if he died that very instant. Lord Mahavira replied,
"If he dies right now, he would go to the seventh hell
on account of his violent state of mind."
After one hour the disciples asked the Lord Mahavira
what would be his destination if he died then.
By this time Prasenjit had realized his error
and had become peaceful inside and out.
Mahavira proclaimed that he would soon be liberated
and would land in heaven.
From a Jain legend.

Gospel reading for the day: Matthew 5:21-37
"Everyone who looks at a woman with lust
has already committed adultery with her in his heart."

Sunday between
February 18 & 24

A reading from the Taoist scriptures:
Recognize the Great in the small,
and the many in the few.
Repay hatred with kindness.
Deal with the difficult while it is still easy.
Begin great works while they are small.
Certainly the Earth does difficult work with ease,
and accomplishes great affairs from small beginnings.
So, the Sage, by not striving for greatness, achieves greatness.
The Way of Heaven does not compete, but is good at winning;
does not speak, yet always responds;
does not demand, but is usually obeyed;
seems chaotic, but unfolds a most excellent plan.
Heaven's net is cast wide,
and though its meshes are loose, nothing is ever lost.
The Tao Te Ching 63, 73

Gospel reading for the day: Matthew 5:38-48
"Love your enemies and pray for those who persecute you."

Sunday between
February 25 & 29

A reading from the Sikh scriptures:
Blessed is the straw hut where God's praises are chanted,
Worthless the white mansions where remembrance of God is not.
Poverty with the holy while contemplating God is bliss itself.
Burn that pride of high state that involves the self with illusion.
Grinding grain with rough clothing brings to the mind
joy and contentment.
What worth kingship without peace of soul?
Adi Granth, Suhi M.5

Gospel reading for the day: Matthew 6:24-34
Do not worry about your life, what you will eat or drink;
or about your body, what you will wear.
Is not life more important than food,
and the body more important than clothes?

Transfiguration
Last Sunday After the Epiphany

A reading from the Islamic scripture:
We have revealed Our will to you as We revealed it to Noah
and to the prophets who came after him;
as We revealed it to Abraham, Ishmael, Isaac, Jacob,
and the tribes; to Jesus, Job, Jonah, Aaron, Solomon,
and David, to whom We gave the Psalms. Of some apostles
We have already told you (how Allah spoke directly to Moses);
but there are others of whom We have not yet spoken:
apostles who brought good news to humankind
and admonished them, so that they might have no
plea against Allah after their coming.
Allah is mighty and wise.
Allah Himself bears witness by that which
He has revealed to you
that it has been revealed with His knowledge;
and so do the angels.
There is no better witness than Allah.
Qur'an 4:163-166

Gospel reading for the day: Matthew 17:1-9
Jesus was transfigured, and his face shown like the sun,
and his garments became white as light.

Ash Wednesday
Years ABC

A reading from the Hindu scriptures:
Quietness of mind, silence, self-harmony, loving-kindness,
and a pure heart: this is the harmony of the mind.
This threefold harmony is called pure
when it is practiced with supreme faith
with no desire for a reward and with oneness of soul.
But false austerity, for the sake of reputation,
honour, and reverence, is impure:
it belongs to kings and is unstable and uncertain.
When self-control is self-torture,
due to dullness of the mind,
or when it aims at hurting another,
then self-control is of darkness.
Bhagavad Gita 17:16-19

Gospel reading for the day: Matthew 6:1-6, 16-21
"Whenever you give alms, do not sound a trumpet before you.
…When you pray, do not be like the hypocrites.
…Do not store up for yourselves treasures on earth."

First Sunday in Lent

A reading from the Zoroastrian tradition:
That devil Angra Mainyu rushed out of hell, and commanded
the demon Buiti to destroy the prophet Zarathustra.
Zarathustra chanted,
"The will of the Lord is the Law of holiness;
the riches of good thought shall be given to him who works
in this world for Mazda, and wields according to the will
of the Lord the power He gave him to relieve the poor...
profess the Law of the worshippers of Mazda!"
The demon rushed away and reported,
"I see no way to kill him, so great is the glory
of holy Zarathustra."
Zarathustra went forward, unshaken by the evil spirit,
swinging stones as large as a house.
That devil Angra Mainyu said,
"What are you swinging those large stones at?"
"Oh evil-doer, I will smite the creation of the devil!"
"Do not destroy my creatures, O holy Zarathustra,"
said Angra Mainyu, "Renounce the good Law of the
worshippers of Mazda, and you will gain a great boon,
and be ruler of the nations."
Zarathustra answered, "No! Never will I renounce
the good law of the worshippers of Mazda,
though my body, my life, my soul should burst!"
Adapted from Videvdad 19.1-7

Gospel reading for the day: Matthew 4:1-11
Jesus was led by the Spirit into the desert to be tempted
by the devil. "Away from me, Satan! For it is written,
'Worship the Lord your God, and serve him only.'"

Second Sunday in Lent

A reading from a native American tradition:
Early in the morning just before the sun came up,
I started praying and I heard something.
It seemed like someone was coming.
I looked towards the South and it was the Great Spirit
that was coming in the form of a skeleton.
He came up to me, so I hit him with my Peace Pipe.
Then I went into a coma, and when I came to,
I was standing with my different colored clothes.
"Did you hear what your great Grandfather told you?"
I answered back and said no.
"Everything he told you, you will not know now,
but he will appear and you will hear everything
he said to you when you go back to the sweat lodge."
I wondered who it was that said those words.
And I looked around and I found a bunch of pigeons
that were sitting on a limb,
and they were the ones talking to me.
George Plenty Wolf

Gospel reading for the day: John 3:1-17
"I tell you the truth, no one can see the kingdom of God
unless he is born again.... The wind blows where it
will, you hear its sound, but you cannot tell where it
comes from or where it is going."

Third Sunday in Lent

A reading from the Taoist scriptures:
The Tao is like an empty pitcher,
poured from, but never drained.
Infinitely deep, it is the source of all things.
It blunts the sharp, unties the knotted,
shades the bright, unites with all Dust.
Dimly seen, yet eternally present,
I do not know who gave birth to it,
It is older than any conception of God.
Tao Te Ching, 4

Gospel reading for the day: John 4:5-26 (27-42)
He met a Samaritan woman by a well, and told her,
"If you knew who it is that is saying to you 'Give me a drink,'
you would have asked him, and he would have given you living
water. Everyone who drinks of this water will be thirsty,
but those who drink of the water that I will give them
will never be thirsty."

Fourth Sunday in Lent

A reading from a native African tradition:
You who are so powerful as to enter inside the
small medicine gourd
to shelter yourself from danger,
Have you forgotten your children?
Have you forgotten your wife?
The evil seeds a man sows
shall be reaped by his offspring.
Cruelty, like a troublesome chicken,
is inevitably punished.
However late it is,
the punishment will come when it will.
Yoruba song

Gospel reading for the day: John 9:1-41
"Rabbi, who sinned, this man or his parents, that he
was born blind?" Jesus answered, "Neither this man nor his
parents sinned; he was born blind so that God's works might be
revealed in him."

Fifth Sunday in Lent

A reading from the Hindu scriptures:
Invisible before birth are all beings
and after death invisible again.
They are seen between two unseens.
Why in this truth find sorrow?
...The Spirit that is in all beings
is immortal in them all:
for the death of what cannot die,
cease thou sorrow.
Bhagavad Gita 2:28-29

Gospel reading for the day: John 11:(1-16) 17-45
"Lord, if you had been here, my brother would not have died."
Jesus cried with a loud voice, "Lazarus, come out!"
The dead man came out. "Unbind him, and let him go."

Palm Sunday
Years ABC

A reading from the Shinto tradition:
Within the world
the palace pillar is broad,
but the human heart
should be modest.
From a poem by Moritake Arakida

Gospel reading for the day: Matthew 21:1-11
The disciples brought the donkey and the colt,
and Jesus sat on them. A large crowd went ahead of him,
shouting, "Hosanna to the Son of David!"

Maundy Thursday
Years ABC

A reading from the Buddhist scriptures:
When your view is the same as your teacher's,
you destroy half your teacher's merit.
When your view surpasses your teacher's,
you are worthy to succeed him.
Zen proverb

Gospel reading for the day: John :1:1-17, 31b-35
Jesus washed the disciples' feet.
"If I, your Lord, have washed your feet,
you ought to wash each other's feet as well....
A servant is not greater than his master;
nor is he who is sent greater than he who sent him."

Passion Sunday or Good Friday

A reading from the Taoist scriptures:
In the whole world nothing is softer or weaker than water.
And yet even those who succeed when attacking the hard
and the strong cannot overcome it, because nothing can harm it.
The weak overcomes the strong. The soft conquers the hard.
No one in the world can deny this,
yet no one seems to know how to put it into practice.
Therefore the Sage says, "One who accepts a people's
shame is qualified to rule it.
One who embraces a condemned people
is called the King of the Universe."
Tao Te Ching 78

Gospel reading for the day:
Matthew 26:14-27:66 or John 18:1-19:42
Jesus was tried before Pilate, who offered Jesus or Barabbas
to the crowd for release. "Give us Barabbas!" The soldiers
beat him and mocked him. Simon helped him carry his cross.
At Golgotha he was crucified between two thieves. Jesus cried,
"Why have you forsaken me?" and breathed his last.

Easter

A reading from the Hindu scriptures:
The wise one is not born, nor does he die,
this one has not come from anywhere,
has not become anyone.
Unborn, constant, eternal, primeval, this one
is not slain when the body is slain.
If the slayer thinks that he slays,
if the slain think themselves slain,
neither of them understand.
No one is slain, and no one slays.
Adapted from Katha Upanishad 2:18-19;
Bhagavad Gita, 2:19-20

Gospel reading for the day: John 20:1-18
Mary Magdalene went to the disciples with the news:
"I have seen the Lord!"
And she told them that he had said these things to her.

Second Sunday of Easter

A reading from the Buddhist tradition:
Whatever monk has doubts about the Teacher,
is perplexed, is not convinced, is not sure,
his mind does not incline to ardor,
to continual application, to perseverance, to striving.
This is the first mental barrenness that thus comes
not to be got rid of by him, whose mind does not
incline to ardor,
to continual application, to perseverance, to striving.
And again, this monk has doubts about the Teaching...
has doubts about the Order...has doubts about the training,
is perplexed, is not convinced, is not sure...
his mind does not incline to ardor...to striving.
If these mental barrennesses are not rooted out,
that he should come to growth, expansion,
and maturity in this Teaching and discipline
—such a situation does not occur.
Majjhima Nikaya i.101, Cetokhila Sutta

Gospel reading for the day: John 20:19-31
Thomas said, "Unless I see the nail marks in his hands,
and put my finger where the nails were,
and put my hand into his side, I will not believe it."

Third Sunday of Easter

A reading from the Islamic tradition:
Did We not expand your breast for you
and lift from you your burden,
the burden that weighted down on your back?
Did We not exalt your fame?
So truly with hardship comes ease,
Truly with hardship comes ease.
So when you are empty, labor,
and let your Lord be your Quest.
Qur'an 94

Gospel reading for the day: Luke 24:13-35
The resurrected Jesus walks with two disciples
towards Emmaus.
In the breaking of bread they recognized him,
and he vanished from their sight.
"Did our hearts not burn within us
as he explained the scriptures?"

Fourth Sunday of Easter

A reading from the Sufi tradition:
Muhammed says, "I come before dawn
to chain you and drag you off."
It's amazing, and funny, that you have to be pulled away
from being tortured, pulled out into this Spring garden
but that's the way it is.
Almost everyone must be bound and dragged here.
Only a few come on their own.
Children have to be made to go to school at first.
Then some of them begin to like it. They run to school....
There are two types on the path. Those who come
against their will, the blindly religious people, and those
who obey out of love. The former have ulterior motives.
They want the Midwife near, because she gives them milk.
The others love the Beauty of the Nurse.
The former memorize the proof-texts of conformity,
and repeat them. The latter disappear
into whatever draws them to God.
Both are drawn from the Source.
Any moving's from the Mover.
Any love from the Beloved.
Rumi

Gospel reading for the day: John 10:1-10
"He calls his own sheep by name and leads them out.
But they will never follow a stranger, because they do not
recognize a stranger's voice. I am the gate for the sheep."

Fifth Sunday of Easter

A reading from the Hindu scriptures:
For the salvation of those who are good,
for the destruction of evil in men,
and for the fulfilment of the kingdom of righteousness,
I come to this world in the ages that pass.
He who knows my birth as God
and who knows my sacrifice,
when he leaves his mortal body,
goes no more from death to death,
for he in truth comes to me.
In any way that men love me
in that same way they find my love:
for many are the paths of men,
but they all in the end come to me.
Baghavad Gita 4:8-9, 11

Gospel reading for the day: John 14:1-14
"In my Father's house are many mansions.
I go to prepare a place for you....
No one comes to the Father but by me.....
I am in the Father and the Father is in me....
If in my name you ask me for anything, I will do it."

Sixth Sunday of Easter

A reading from the Baha'i tradition:
Inasmuch as these Birds of the Celestial Throne
are all sent down from the heaven of the Will of God,
and as they all arise to proclaim His irresistible Faith,
they therefore are regarded as one soul and the same person.
For they all drink from the one Cup of the love of God,
and all partake of the fruit of the same Tree of Oneness.
These Manifestations of God have each a twofold station.
One is the nation of pure abstraction and essential unity.
In this respect, if you call them all by one name,
and ascribe to them the same attribute,
you have not erred from the truth.
Even as he has revealed, "No distinction do We make
between any of His Messengers!"
For they one and all summon the people of the earth
to acknowledge the Unity of God.
Book of Certitude, 152, 176

Gospel reading for the day: John 14:15-21
"If you love me you will keep my commandments.
And I will ask the Father, and he will give you another
Advocate, to be with you forever."

Seventh Sunday of Easter

A reading from the Jewish tradition:

Wisdom says, "I came forth from the mouth of the Most High, and covered the earth like a mist. I dwelt in the highest heavens, and my throne was in a pillar of cloud. Alone I compassed the vault of heaven and traversed the depths of the abyss. Over waves of the sea, over all the earth, and over every people and nation I have held sway. Among all these I sought a resting place; in whose territory should I abide? Then the Creator of all things gave me a command, and my Creator chose the place for my tent. He said, 'Make your dwelling in Jacob, and in Israel receive your inheritance....' I am the mother of beautiful love, of fear, of knowledge, and of holy hope; being eternal, I am given to all my children, to those who are named by him. Come to me, you who desire me, and eat your fill of my fruits. For the memory of me is sweeter than honey, and the possession of me sweeter than the honeycomb. Those who eat of me will hunger for more, and those who drink of me will thirst for more. Whoever obeys me will not be put to shame, and those who work with me will not sin."

Ecclesiasticus 24

Gospel reading for the day: John 17:1-11
"All I have is yours...all glory has come to me through them.
I will remain in the world no longer, but they are still in the
World.... Protect them so that they may be one as we are one."

Ascension
Years ABC

A reading from the Buddhist tradition:
The Buddha turned to his disciples and said to them:
"Everything comes to an end.
I have done what I could do, both for myself and others.
To stay here would from now on be without any purpose.
Hereafter my teaching shall abide for generations.
Therefore, recognize the true nature of the living
world, and do not be anxious; for separation
cannot possibly be avoided.
Recognize that all that lives is subject to this law;
and strive from today that it shall be thus no more!
Everything is bound to perish in the end.
Be ye therefore mindful and vigilant!
The time for my entry into Nirvana has now arrived!
These are my last words!"
And when the Sage entered Nirvana,
the earth quivered like a ship struck by a storm,
and fire fell from the sky.
Parinirvana

Gospel reading for the day: John 14:15-21
"If you love me you will keep my commandments.
And I will ask the Father, and he will give you
another Advocate, to be with you forever."

Pentecost

A reading from the Zoroastrian scriptures:
Seek to glorify him for us with hymns of devotion,
him who is beheld in the soul as the Wise Lord,
because he has promised with his
Righteousness and his Good Mind
that integrity and immortality shall be ours in his dominion,
strength and endurance in his house!
As the holy one I recognized thee, O Wise Lord.
When he came to me as Good Mind;
the Silent Thought taught me the greatest good,
so that I might proclaim it.
Avesta, Yasna 45:10, 15

Gospel reading for the day: John 20:19-23
"Peace be with you! As the Father has sent me,
I am sending you." And with that he breathed
on them and said, "Receive the Holy Spirit."

Trinity Sunday
First Sunday after Pentecost

A reading from the Wiccan tradition:
Set sail, set sail, follow the twilight to the West,
where you may rest, where you may rest.
Set sail, set sail, turn your face where the sun grows dim,
beyond the rim, beyond the rim.
Set sail, set sail, one thing becomes another
in the Mother, in the Mother.
Set sail, set sail, make of your heart a burning fire,
build it higher, build it higher.
Set sail, set sail, pass in an instant through the open gate,
it will not wait, it will not wait.
Set sail, set sail, over the dark of the sunless sea,
you are free, you are free.
Set sail, set sail, guide the ship of the rising sun,
you are the one, you are the one.
Set sail, set sail, into the raging wind and storm,
to be reborn, to be reborn.
Set sail, set sail, over the waves where the spray blows white,
to bring the light, to bring the light.
Spiral Dance, 183-4

Gospel reading for the day: Matthew 28:16-20
"Go therefore and make disciples of all nations,
baptizing them in the name of the Father
and of the Son and of the Holy Spirit....
I am with you always, to the end of the age."

Sunday between
May 29 and June 4

Use only if after Trinity Sunday

A reading from the Islamic scripture:
Have you not seen how God has struck a similitude?
A good word is as a good tree—its roots are firm,
and its branches are in heaven;
it gives its produce every season by the leave of its Lord.
So God strikes similitudes for men; haply they will remember.
And the likeness of a corrupt word is as a corrupt tree—
uprooted from the earth, having no establishment.
God confirms those who believe with him the firm word,
in the present life and in the world to come;
and God leads astray the evildoers; and God does what He will.
Qur'an 14:24-27

Gospel reading for the day: Matthew 7:21-29
"Whoever hears my words and does them
will be like a wise man who built his house upon the rock...."

Sunday between June 5 & 11

Use only if after Trinity Sunday

A reading from the Jewish tradition:
Once, as Rabbi Yohanan ben Zakkai
was coming forth from Jerusalem,
Rabbi Joshua followed after him and beheld the Temple in ruins.
"Woe unto us," Rabbi Joshua cried, "that this, the place
where the iniquities of Israel were atoned for, is laid waste!"
"My son," Rabbi Yohanan said to him, "be not grieved.
We have another atonement as effective as this.
And what is it? It is acts of loving-kindness,
as it is said, 'For I desire mercy and not sacrifice.'"
Talmud, Abot de Rabbi Nathan 6

Gospel reading for the day: Matthew 9:9-13, 18-26
The Pharisees asked the disciples,
"Why does your teacher eat with tax collectors and sinners?"
"Those who are well have no need of a physician.
I have come to call not the righteous, but sinners."
Jesus healed the woman suffering from hemorrhages,
"Your faith has made you well."

Sunday between June 12 & 18

Use only if after Trinity Sunday

A reading from the Buddhist scripture:
Then the Exalted One said to the brethren,
"I am released, brethren, from all conditions,
those that are divine and those that are human.
You also, brethren, are released from all bonds,
those that are divine and those that are human.
Go forth, brethren, on your journey, for the profit of the many,
for the bliss of the many, out of compassion for the world,
for the welfare, the profit, the bliss of gods and humans!
Go not any two together. Proclaim, brethren, the Norm,
goodly in its beginning, goodly in its middle, goodly in its ending.
Both in the spirit and in the letter make
known the all-perfected, utterly pure righteous life.
There are beings with but little dust of passion on their eyes.
They are perishing through not hearing the Norm.
There will be some who will understand."
Vinaya Pitaka i.21

Gospel reading for the day: Matthew 9:35-10:8
"Go to the lost sheep of the house of Israel.
As you go, proclaim the good news...cure the sick,
raise the dead, cleanse the lepers, cast out demons."

Sunday between June 19 & 25

Use only if after Trinity Sunday

A reading from a native African tradition:
The goddess of the sea says goodbye,
She-who-carries-loads-and-never-looks-back.
Since this is how we find the world,
we must fight.
The world has not peace;
this is war.
We must fight to the last man
so that the world may have peace.
Yoruban War Song

Gospel reading for the day: Matthew 10:34-42
"Do not think that I have come to bring peace to the earth;
I have not come to bring peace, but a sword."

Sunday between
June 26 & July 2

A reading from the Shinto tradition:
Those who do not abandon mercy
Will not be abandoned by me.
Oracle of Itsukushima

Gospel reading for the day: Matthew 10:40-42
"If anyone gives even a cup of cold water to one of these
little ones because he is my disciple, he will certainly
not lose his reward."

Sunday between July 3 & 9

A reading from the Buddhist scriptures:
I am the Tathagata, the Worshipful, the All-wise,
the Perfectly Enlightened in Conduct, the Well-departured,
the Understander of the world,
the Peerless Leader, the Controller,
the Teacher of Gods and Men, the Buddha, the World-honored
One. Those who have not yet been saved, I cause to be saved;
those who have not yet been set free, to be set free;
those who have not yet been comforted, to be comforted;
those who have not yet obtained Nirvana, to obtain Nirvana.
I know the present world and the world to come
as they really are.
I am the All-knowing, the All-seeing, the Knower of the Way,
the Opener of the Way, the Preacher of the Way.
Come to me, all you gods, men, and demons, to hear the Law.
Lotus Sutra 5

Gospel reading for the day: Matthew 11:25–30
"Come to me, all you that are weary and are
carrying heavy burdens, and I will give you rest."

Sunday between July 10 & 16

A reading from the Taoist scriptures:
When wise people hear about the Tao,
they follow it carefully.
When ordinary people hear about the Tao,
they can take it or leave it.
When foolish people hear about the Tao,
they laugh out loud.
If they didn't laugh out loud,
it wouldn't be the Tao!
Tao Te Ching 65

Gospel reading for the day: Matthew 13:1-9, 18-23
"When anyone hears the message about the kingdom
and does not understand it, the evil one comes
and snatches away what has been sown in his heart."

Sunday between July 17 & 23

A reading from the Confucian tradition:
Feng said, "Everyone who commits crime—stealing, dishonesty
and treachery, murder, assault, and recklessness
—these are abhorrent to everybody."
The king answered, "Feng, such people are indeed abhorred,
as well as those who do not respect his father with reverence.
He breaks his father's heart, and the father can
no longer love his son, but hates him instead.
Or the younger brother who does not consider
the will of Heaven, and does not respect his elder brother;
the elder brother who does not consider the sacrifices of his
parents in raising him and treats his brother unkindly.
If we who are responsible to govern do not treat such people,
who continue to be wicked, as offenders, the laws given to us
by Heaven will be thrown into chaos and destroyed.
You must resolve to deal expeditiously with such people
according to the penal code, punishing them severely,
and showing no mercy."
Book of History, 5.9

Gospel reading for the day: Matthew 13:24-30, 36-43
"The Kingdom of heaven is like a man who sowed good seed in
his field; his enemy came and sowed weeds among the wheat.
His servants said, 'Sir, do you want us to pull up the weeds?'
'No, let both grow together until the harvest.'"

Sunday between July 24 & 30

A reading from the Zoroastrian scriptures:
Hear with your ears that which is the sovereign good;
with a clear mind look upon the two sides
between which each man must choose for himself,
watchful beforehand that the great test
may be accomplished in our favor.
Now at the beginning the twin spirits have declared
their nature, the better and the evil,
in thought and word and deed.
And between the two
the wise ones choose well,
not the foolish.
Avesta, Yasna 30.2-3

Gospel reading for the day: Matthew 13:44-52
"The kingdom of heaven is like a merchant
who finds a pearl of great value."

Sunday between
July 31 & August 6

A reading from the Buddhist scriptures:
Because I see danger in the practice of miracles,
I loathe and abhor and repudiate them.
Digha Nikaya xi.66, Kevadddha Sutta

Gospel reading for the day: Matthew 14:13-21
Taking the loaves and fishes, he gave thanks
and broke the loaves.
They all ate and were satisfied, the number of those who
ate was about five thousand men, besides women and children.

Sunday between August 7 & 13

A reading from the Sikh tradition:
Through faith man meets no obstacle on the Path,
and shall proceed to his abode with God
with his honor universally proclaimed....
Through faith man finds the Door of Liberation:
even his relatives are liberated through him....
Says Nanak, One with faith
need not wander about begging for divine grace.
The great, immaculate Name of God
may only be realized by one
whose mind is firmly fixed in faith.
Adi Granth, Japuji 12-15, M.1, p. 3

Gospel reading for the day: Matthew 14:22-33
Jesus came to them, walking on the sea.
So Peter got out of the boat and walked on the water,
but when he saw the wind he was afraid.
"O man of little faith, why did you doubt?"

Sunday between
August 14 & 20

A reading from the Jain scriptures:
Some shameless men, becoming monks,
propagate a doctrine of their own. And others believe in it,
put their faith in it, adopt it, saying,
"Well, you speak the truth, O Brahmin!
We shall present you with food, drink, spices,
and sweetmeats, with a robe, a bowl, or a broom."
Some have induced others to honor them,
and some have made their proselytes to honor them.
Before, they were determined to become genuine holy men,
poor monks who would have neither sons nor cattle,
to eat only what should be given them by others,
and to commit no sins.
But after having entered the religious life they do not cease
from committing sins, they cause others to commit sins,
and they assent to another's committing sins.
Thus they are given to pleasures, amusements,
and sensual lust; they are greedy, fettered, passionate,
covetous, the slaves of love and hate;
therefore they cannot free themselves
nor free anyone else.
Sutrakritanga 2.1.18-19

Gospel reading for the day: Matthew 15: (10-20) 21-28
"What goes into a man's mouth does not
make him 'unclean,' but what comes out of his mouth,
that is what makes him 'unclean.'"

Sunday between
August 21 & 27

A reading from the Sikh scriptures:
Immutable is the city of the Divine Master,
wherein those contemplating the Name attain joy.
In this city founded by the Creator
are fulfilled desires of the heart:
The Lord has founded it; all joys are obtained herein.
To our progeny, brothers and disciples
has come the bloom of joy.
As they sing praise of the Lord,
perfection incarnate,
their objectives are fulfilled.
Adi Granth, Suhi Chant M.5

Gospel reading for the day: Matthew 16:13-20
"On this rock I will build my church,
and the powers of death shall not prevail against it."

Sunday between
August 28 and September 3

A reading from the Confucian scriptures:
Mencius said, "Fish is what I want;
bear's palm is also what I want.
If I cannot have both, I would rather take the
bear's palm than fish.
Life is what I want; dutifulness is also what I want.
If I cannot have both, I would rather take dutifulness than life.
On the one hand, though life is what I want,
there is something I want more than life.
That is why I do not cling to life at all costs.
On the other hand, though death is what I loathe,
there is something I loathe more than death.
That is why there are troubles I do not avoid.
If there is nothing a man wants more than life,
then why should he have scruples about any means,
so long as it will serve to keep him alive?"
Mencius VI.A.10

Gospel reading for the day: Matthew 16:21-28
"If any man would come after me,
let him deny himself and take up his cross and follow me."

Sunday between
September 4 & 10

A reading from the Islamic tradition:
And when a company meets together
in one of the houses of God
to pore over the Book of God
and to study it together among themselves,
the Shechinah comes down to them
and mercy overshadows them,
and angels surround them
and God remembers them among them that are His.
Forty Hadith of an-Nawawi 36

Gospel reading for the day: Matthew 18:15-20
"Where two or three are gathered in my name,
there am I in the midst of them."

Sunday between
September 11 & 17

A reading from the Jewish tradition:
How is one proved a repentant sinner?
Rab Judah said, "If the object which
caused his original transgression comes before him
on two occasions, and he keeps away from it."
Rabbi Jose ben Judah said,
"If a man commits a transgression,
the first, second, and third time he is forgiven;
the fourth time he is not forgiven."
Talmud, Yoma 86b

Gospel reading for the day: Matthew 18:21-35
"Lord how often shall my brother sin against me,
and I forgive him?"

Sunday between
September 18 & 24

A reading from the Islamic tradition:
Allah the Almighty has said, "O son of Adam,
so long as you call upon Me and ask of Me,
I shall forgive you for what you have done,
and I shall not mind.
"O son of Adam, were your sins to reach the clouds
of the sky and were you to then ask forgiveness of Me,
I would forgive you. O son of Adam,
were you to come to Me with sins
nearly as great as the earth and were you to then face Me,
ascribing no partner to Me,
I would bring you forgiveness nearly as great as the earth."
Forty Hadith of an-Nawawi 42

Gospel reading for the day: Matthew 20:1-16
"Friend, I am not being unfair to you. Didn't you agree to work
for a denarius? Take your pay and go. I want to give the man
who was hired last the same as I gave you. Don't I have the right
to do what I want with my own money?"

Sunday between
September 25 & October 1

A reading from the Hindu tradition:
Many are the gurus who are proficient to the utmost
in Vedas and Shastras; but rare is the guru
who has attained to the supreme Truth.
Many are the gurus on earth who give
what is other than the Self;
but rare is the guru who brings to light the Atman.
Many are the gurus who rob the disciple of his wealth;
but rare is the guru who removes the people's afflictions.
Many are they who are given to the discipline and conduct
according to caste, stage, and family;
but he who is devoid of all volition is a guru rare to find.
He is the guru by whose very contact
there flows the supreme bliss;
the intelligent man shall choose such a one
as the guru and no other.
Kularnava Tantra 13

Gospel reading for the day: Matthew 21:23-32
"A man had two sons; he went to the first and said, 'Go and
work in the vineyard.' 'No,' the son answered, but later changed
his mind and went. Then the father went to the other son and
said the same thing. This son said, 'I will' but did not go.
Which of the two did what his father wanted?"

Sunday between October 2 & 8

A reading from the native African tradition:
On us shall descend some awful curse,
like the curse that descended in far-off times.
Thus speaks the Creator of men,
but the men refuse to listen.
On us shall descend some awful curse,
like the curse that descended in far-off times,
we have but one word to say:
Idle about! Sink in sloth!
Men of such kind will gain another from the Father,
for they know not his voice.
He is the one who loves human beings.
Dinka Prayer, Sudan

Gospel reading for the day: Matthew 21:33-46
"The kingdom of God will be taken away from you and
given to a people who will produce its fruit."

Sunday between October 9 & 15

A reading from the Jewish scriptures:
On this mountain the Lord of hosts will make for all peoples
a feast of rich food, a feast of well-aged wines,
of rich food filled with marrow,
of well-aged wines strained clear.
And he will destroy on this mountain
the shroud that is cast over all the peoples,
the sheet that is spread over all nations;
he will swallow up death forever.
The Lord God will wipe away the tears from all faces,
and the disgrace of his people he will take away
from all the earth,
For the Lord has spoken.
Isaiah 24: 6-8

Gospel reading for the day: Matthew 22:1-14
"The kingdom of heaven is like a king who prepared
a wedding banquet for his son. He sent his servants to those
who had been invited, but they refused to come.
'Go to the street corners and invite to the banquet
anyone you find.'"

Sunday between
October 16 & 22

A reading from the Taoist tradition:
Do not race after riches,
do not risk your life for success,
or you will let slip the Heaven within you.
Chuang Tzu 29

Gospel reading for the day: Matthew 22:15-22
"Give to Caesar what is Caesar's, and to God what is God's."

Sunday between
October 23 & 29

A reading from the Jewish tradition:
A certain heathen came to Shammai and said to him,
"Make me a convert, on condition that you teach me
the whole Torah while I stand on one foot."
Thereupon Shammai drove him away with a stick.
When the man went to Hillel and made the same request,
he was told, "What is hateful to you, do not do to your neighbor:
that is the whole Torah; all the rest is commentary.
Go and learn."
Talmud, Shabbat 31a

Gospel reading for the day: Matthew 22:34-46
"You shall love the Lord your God with all your heart,
and with all your soul, and with all your mind.
This is the greatest and first commandment."

Sunday between
October 30 & November 5

A reading from the Buddhist scriptures:
As a flower that is lovely and beautiful,
but is scentless, even so fruitless is the well-spoken word
of one who does not practice it.
As a flower that is lovely, beautiful, and scent-laden,
even so fruitful is the well-spoken word
of one who practices it.
Dhammapada 51-52

Gospel reading for the day: Matthew 23:1-12
"The scribes and the Pharisees sit on Moses' seat;
so practice and observe whatever they tell you,
but not what they do; for they preach, but do not practice."

All Saints Day
November 1 or First Sunday in November

A reading from the Taoist scriptures:
What do I mean by a True Human Being?
The True Human Beings of ancient times
did not rebel against want,
did not grow proud in plenty, and did not plan their affairs.
Being like this, they could commit errors and not regret it,
could meet with success and not make a show....
The True Human Beings of ancient times knew nothing
of loving life, knew nothing of hating death.
They emerged without delight;
they went back in without a fuss.
They came briskly, they went briskly, and that was all.
They did not forget where they began,
and did not try to find out where they would end.
They received something and took pleasure in it;
they forgot about it and handed it back again.
This is what I call not using the mind to repel the Way.
Chuang Tzu 6

Gospel reading for the day: Matthew 5:1-12
"Blessed are the peacemakers,
for they shall be called the children of God."

Sunday between
November 6 & 12

A reading from the Jain scriptures:
Though others sleep, be thou awake!
Like a wise man, trust nobody, but be always on the alert;
for dangerous is the time and weak the body.
Be as watchful as the two-headed bharaunda bird!
A monk should step carefully in his walk,
supposing everything to be a snare for him.
First, he must bestow care on his life till he wins Enlightenment,
and afterwards he should despise his body, annihilating its sins.
Uttaradhyayana Sutra 4:6-7

Gospel reading for the day: Matthew 25:1-13
Ten bridesmaids await the bridegroom.
Five of them take full containers of oil for their lamps,
but the other five neglect to take any oil.

Sunday between
November 13 & 19

A reading from the Hindu scriptures:
In the dark night live those for whom
the world without alone is real;
in night darker still live those
for whom the world within alone is real.
The first leads to a life of action,
the second to a life of meditation.
But those who combine action with meditation
cross the sea of death through action
and enter into immortality
through the practice of meditation.
So have we heard from the wise.
Isha Upanishad 9-11

Gospel reading for the day: Matthew 23:1-12
Three servants were entrusted with talents.
Two of them showed a return on their master's investment,
but one buried his talent in the earth.

Christ the King
Sunday between November 20 & 26

A reading from the Islamic tradition:
On the day of judgement God Most High will say,
"Son of Adam, I was sick and you did not visit Me."
He will reply, "My Lord, how could I visit Thee
when Thou art the Lord of the Universe!"
He will say, "Did you not know
that my servant so-and-so was ill
and yet you did not visit him?
Did you not know that if you had visited him
you soon would have found Me with him?"
Hadith of Muslim

Gospel reading for the day: Matthew 25:31-46
Before him will be gathered all the nations,
and he will separate them one from another
as a shepherd separates the sheep from the goats.

Thanksgiving Day
Fourth Thursday in November

A reading from the Taoist scriptures:
There is no greater curse than discontent.
Nothing breeds trouble like greed.
Only one who is content with enough will be content always....
Forget "holiness," abandon "intelligence,"
and people will be a hundred times better off.
Give up "humanitarianism," put away "righteousness,"
and people will rediscover brotherly love and kindness.
Forget "great art," throw away "profit"
and there will be no more thieves.
These things are superficial and are simply not enough.
People need something solid to hold on to.
And here it is: Be real. Embrace simplicity.
Put others first. Desire little.
Tao Te Ching 46, 19

Gospel reading for the day: Matthew 6:25-33
"Don't worry about your life, what you will eat or what you will
drink, or about your body, what you will wear. Is not life more
than food, and the body more than clothing?"

Year B

First Sunday in Advent

A reading from the Hindu tradition:
Wealth and piety will decrease day by day, until the world will be totally depraved. Then property alone will confer rank; wealth will be the only source of devotion; passion will be the sole bond of union between the sexes; falsehood will be the only means of success in litigation; and women will be objects merely of sensual gratification. Earth will be venerated but for its mineral treasures; priestly vestments will constitute a priest...menace and presumption will be substituted for learning; liberality will be devotion; simple ablutions will be purification; mutual assent will be marriage; fine clothes will be dignity; and water afar off will be esteemed a holy spring.... The people, unable to bear the heavy burdens imposed upon them by their avaricious sovereigns, will take refuge amongst the valleys of the mountains...their only covering will be the bark of trees, and they will be exposed to the cold and wind and sun and rain. No one's life will exceed twenty-three years. Thus in the Kali age shall decay constantly proceed, until the human race approaches its annihilation.

Vishnu Purana 4.24

Gospel reading for the day: Mark 13:24-37
"In those days, the sun will be darkened, the stars will fall from the sky.... At that time men will see the Son of Man coming in clouds with great power and glory. So, watch!"

Second Sunday in Advent

A reading from the Islamic scriptures:
And remember Jesus, the son of Mary, said,
"O Children of Israel! I am the apostle of God to you,
confirming the Law which came before me,
and giving glad tidings of an apostle to come after me
whose name shall be Ahmad."
But when he came to them with clear signs,
they said, "This is evident sorcery."
Qur'an 61.6

Gospel reading for the day: Mark 1:1-8
John came, baptizing in the desert and preaching a
baptism of repentance, "After me will come one
more powerful than I...."

Third Sunday in Advent

A reading from the Jewish tradition:
When Abraham saw the sun issuing in the morning
from the east, he was first moved to think that it was God,
and said, "This is the King that created me,"
and worshipped it the whole day.
In the evening when the sun went down and the moon
commenced to shine, he said, "Verily this rules over the orb
which I worshipped the whole day, since the latter is
darkened before it and does not shine any more."
So he served the moon all that night.
In the morning when he saw the darkness depart
and the east grow light, he said, "Of a surety there is a
King who rules over all these orbs and orders them."
Zohar, Genesis 86a

Gospel reading for the day: Mark 1:6-8, 19-28
John said, "I am not the Christ." "Then who are you?
Are you Elijah? Are you the prophet?" "No," he told them,
"I am the voice of one calling in the desert, 'Make straight
the way of the Lord.'"

Fourth Sunday in Advent

A reading from the Islamic tradition:

In the month of Ramadan, Muhammad set forth to Hira, and his family with him. The angel Gabriel came to him while he was asleep. The angel pointed at the brocade coverlet the Apostle was sleeping under, which was covered in writing. "Read!" the angel commanded. "I cannot read," the Apostle protested.... "What shall I read?" Muhammad asked him. He replied, "Read! In the name of thy Lord who created humankind out of blood. Read! The Lord is beneficent, who taught by the pen, taught that which was unknown to humans."

Muhammad read it, and the angel departed from him, but it was as if the angel's words were written upon his heart. "None of God's creatures are more hateful to me than an ecstatic poet or a man possessed," Muhammad said, "So I thought, Woe is me, never shall anyone say of me he is a poet or possessed!" Muhammad was so distraught he went to kill himself by throwing himself off of a mountain. But then he heard a voice from heaven saying, "O Muhammad! Thou art the Apostle of God and I am Gabriel."

When Muhammad told his wife what had happened she insisted he visit her cousin Waraqa, a Christian who studied the Torah and the Gospel. When Waraqa heard what had happened, he cried, "Holy! Holy! Holy! Verily by Him in whose hand is Waraqa's soul, if you have spoken the truth, there came to him the greatest angel, Gabriel, who came to Moses before us and lo, Muhammad is the prophet of this people."

Adapted from Sirat Rasul Allah

Gospel reading for the day: Luke: 1:26-38
The angel Gabriel appeared to Mary and announced that she
will bear a son.

Christmas | Same as reading for Year A

First Sunday after Christmas

A reading from a native African tradition:
Brothers and sisters, a new child is born.
While in the womb it belonged to its mother;
safely delivered, it is everybody's child.
He shall grow up cared for by his parents, and
when is grown he will look after them.
He should not follow what is wrong.
We want genuinely good children,
not just any children.
He will grow up industrious,
he will be like his father, his mother,
and his other relatives.
Adapted from Igbo Naming Ceremony—Nigeria

Gospel reading for the day: Luke 2:22-40
Simeon praised God, saying, "Lord, as you promised,
let your servant go in peace.
For I have seen your salvation,
which you have prepared for all the world to see."

Holy Name of Jesus
Same as reading for Year A

New Year's Day
Same as reading for Year A

Second Sunday after Christmas
Same as reading for Year A

Epiphany
Same as reading for Year A

Baptism of the Lord

A reading from the Sikh tradition:
Nearly 500 years ago, a herdsman named Nanak
went missing for three days.
He had been bathing,
and it was said that he probably had drowned.
But he did not drown. Instead,
he had been in the presence of the Primal Being....
A cup of nectar was given to him, and he was told,
"Nanak, this is the cup of name-adoration.
Drink it, and go forth rejoicing in My Name.
Teach others to rejoice in My Name.
I have imparted to you the gift of My Name.
This is your vocation."
When he returned from the river,
he sat in meditation for a whole day.
When he finally spoke, he said,
"There is no Hindu. There is no Muslim."
Adapted from The Name of My Beloved

Gospel reading for the day: Mark 1:4-11
Jesus was baptized by John in the Jordan.
As Jesus was coming out of the water, a voice came from
heaven, "You are my son...with you I am well pleased."

Sunday between
January 14 & 20

A reading from the Buddhist tradition:
At one time the Lord was journeying
along the highroad between Ukkatha and Setabbya;
so also was the Brahmin Dona.
He saw on the Lord's footprints the wheels
with their thousand spokes, their rims and hubs
and all their attributes complete, and he thought,
"Indeed, how wonderful and marvelous—
it cannot be that these are the footprints
of a human being."
Anguttara Nikaya ii. 37a

Gospel reading for the day: John 1:43-50
When Jesus saw Nathanael approaching, he said,
"I saw you under the fig tree."
Nathanael declared, "Rabbi, you are the Son of God."
Jesus said, "You believe because I told you I saw you under
the fig tree. You shall see greater things than that."

Sunday between
January 21 & 27

A reading from the Confucian tradition:
The master said,
"Only one who bursts with eagerness do I instruct;
only one who bubbles with excitement do I enlighten.
If I hold up one corner and a man cannot come back to me
with the other three, I do not continue the lesson."
Analects 7.8

Gospel reading for the day: Mark 1:14-20
"Come, follow me," Jesus said, "and I will make you fishers of
men." At once they left their nets, and followed him.

Sunday between
January 28 & February 3

A reading from the Buddhist scriptures:
The Essence of Mind is the real Buddha,
while heretical views and greed, anger, and delusion
are Mara, the evil One.
Enlightened by right views,
we call forth the Buddha within us.
When our nature is dominated by greed, anger, or delusion,
we are said to be possessed by the Devil;
but when right views eliminate from our mind
these poisonous elements
the devil will be transformed into a real Buddha.
Sutra of Hui Neng 10

Gospel reading for the day: Mark 1:21-28
A possessed man cried out, "What do you want with us, Jesus?"
"Be quiet!" Jesus said sternly, "Come out of him!"

Presentation I February 2 I Same as Year A

Sunday between
February 11 & 17

A reading from the Buddhist tradition:
For the sake of the King,
the World-honored One entered into deep meditation.
When he reached the state of samadhi, a great light shone out.
The light was clear and cool,
and it struck the king and shone upon his body.
The boils on his body healed up,
and his choking and pain diminished.
Feeling relieved and peaceful,
the king said to the Buddha,
"Where does this light come from?
It shines on me and touches me;
it cures all boils, and the body feels peace."
The Buddha answered, "O great king!
This is the light of the heaven of heavens.
This light has no root; it is boundless.
It is seen only where there is a desire to save....
O King, you said before that there was no good doctor
in the world who could cure the body and mind.
Because of this, this light is first sent out.
It first cures your body, and then, your mind."
Mahaparinirvana Sutra 575-76

Gospel reading for the day: Mark 1:40-45
A man with leprosy begged him,
"If you are willing, you can make me clean."

Sunday between
February 18 & 24

A reading from the Jewish scriptures:
Come, let us return to the Lord;
for he has torn, that he may heal us;
he has stricken, and he will bind us up.
After two days he will revive us;
on the third day he will raise us up,
that we may live before him.
Hosea 6:1-2

Gospel reading for the day: Mark 2:1-12
When Jesus saw their faith, he said to the paralytic,
"Son, your sins are forgiven." Some of the teachers of the law
said, "Why does this fellow talk like that? He's blaspheming!"

Sunday between
February 25 & 29

A reading from the Sikh scriptures:
Should one perform a million ritual acts and of these be proud,
they leave him only fatigued, and are of little avail.
One who performs innumerable austerities
and for these bears pride,
shall remain caught in transmigration,
moving between heaven and hell.
With all a man's effort, should his self not turn compassionate,
how may he have access to the Divine Portal?
Adi Granth, Gauri Sukhmani M.5

Gospel reading for the day: Mark 2:13-22
Some people asked Jesus,
"How is it that John's disciples and the disciples of the
Pharisees are fasting, but yours are not?"

Transfiguration of the Lord
Sunday preceding Lent

A reading from the Hindu scriptures:
Parvati saw her son Ganesha alive again,
and embraced him with great joy.
She put new clothes on him, and after kissing him, she said,
"Genesha, you have had great tribulation since your birth.
But now you are blessed and content.
You will receive worship before all the gods,
and will be free of distress...."
Shiva, Brahma, and Vishnu declared in unison,
"O great gods, just as we three are worshipped
in all the three worlds, so also Ganesha
shall be worshipped by all of you.
He is the remover of obstacles
and the bestower of the fruits of all rites."
Shiva Purana, Rudrasamhita 18

Gospel reading for the day: Mark 9:2-9
Jesus was transfigured on a high mountain.
His clothes became dazzling white, and Elijah and Moses
appeared before them, talking to Jesus.

Ash Wednesday | Same as reading for Year A

First Sunday in Lent

A reading from the Sikh scriptures:
I, an idle bard, by Thee a task am assigned:
In primal time was I commanded night and day to laud Thee.
The bard was summoned by the Master to the Eternal Mansion,
and was honored with the robe of divine laudation and praise.
On the holy Name ambrosial was he feasted.
As by the Master's guidance on this he has feasted,
has felt blessed.
The bard has spread and proclaimed divine laudation
by the holy Word.
Says Nanak, By laudation of the holy Eternal
is the Supreme Being, all-perfection, attained.
Adi Granth, Var Majh M.1

Gospel reading for the day: Mark 1:9-14
Jesus was baptized, and tempted by Satan. Then he went into
Galilee, proclaiming the Good News of God.

Second Sunday in Lent

A reading from the Jewish tradition:
If the Holy One is pleased with a man,
he crushes him with painful sufferings....
Now, you might think that this is so
even if he did not accept them with love.
Therefore it is said, "To see if his soul
would offer itself in restitution."
Even as the trespass offering must be brought by consent,
so also the sufferings must be endured with consent.
And if he did accept them, what is his reward?
"He will see his seed, prolong his days."
And more than that, his knowledge of Torah
will endure with him. For it is said,
"The purpose of the Lord will prosper in his hand."
Talmud, Berakot 5a

Gospel reading for the day: Mark 8:31-37
He taught them that the Son of Man must suffer many things.
"Whoever wants to save his life will lose it, but whoever loses
his life for me and for the Gospel will save it."

Third Sunday in Lent

A reading from the Sikh scriptures:
Invincible is the army of the Saints.
Great warriors are they; humility is their breastplate;
the songs of the Lord's glory are their weapons;
the word of the Guru is their buckler.
They ride the horses, chariots, and elephants
of the understanding of the Divine Path.
Without fear, they advance towards the enemy.
They ride into battle singing the Lord's praise.
By conquering those five robber chiefs, the vices,
they find that they have also conquered the whole world.
Adi Granth, Shalok Sehskriti M.5

Gospel reading for the day: John 2:13-22
Jesus is enraged by the moneychangers in the temple.
"Stop making my Father's house a marketplace!"

Fourth Sunday in Lent

A reading from the Islamic tradition:
I asked Mohammed,
the Messenger of God,
"Did you see your Lord?"
He said,
"He is a Light,
how could I see Him?"
Hadith of Muslim

Gospel reading for the day: John 3:14-21
God so loved the world that he gave his one and only Son.
Light has come into the world, but men loved darkness instead.

Fifth Sunday in Lent

A reading from the Seicho-n-Ie scriptures:
Humanity's real nature is primarily spiritual life,
which weaves its threads of mind to build a cocoon of flesh,
encloses its own soul in the cocoon,
and for the first time, the spirit becomes flesh.
Understand this clearly: the cocoon is not the silkworm;
in the same way, the physical body is not a human being
but merely a human being's cocoon.
Just as the silkworm will break out of its cocoon and fly free,
so, too, will a person break out of the body-cocoon
and ascend to the spiritual world when his or her time is come.
Never think that the death of the physical body
is the death of a person.
Since humans are life, they will never know death.
Nectarean Shower of Holy Doctrines

Gospel reading for the day: John 12:20-33
"Unless a kernel of wheat falls to the ground and dies,
it remains only a single seed. But if it dies,
it produces many seeds."

Maundy Thursday
Same as Year A

Palm Sunday
Same as Year A

Passion Sunday or Good Friday
Same as Year A

Easter

A reading from a native African tradition:
Those who are dead are never gone;
they are there in the thickening shadow.
The dead are not under the earth:
they are there in the tree that rustles,
they are in the wood that groans,
they are in the water that runs,
they are in the water that sleeps,
they are in the hut, they are in the crowd,
the dead are not dead.
Those who are dead are never gone:
they are in the breast of the woman,
they are in the child who is wailing,
and in the firebrand that flames.
The dead are not under the earth:
they are in the fire that is dying,
they are in the grasses that weep,
they are in the whimpering rocks,
they are in the forest, they are in the house,
the dead are not dead.
Birago Diop, Mali Poem

Gospel reading for the day: John 20:1-18
Mary Magdalene went to the tomb and saw that the stone
had been removed. "They have taken the Lord out of the tomb,
and we don't know where they have put him!"

Second Sunday of Easter

A reading from the Hindu scriptures:
A man of faith, absorbed in faith, his senses controlled,
attains knowledge, and, knowledge attained,
quickly finds supreme peace. But the ignorant man,
who is without faith, goes doubting to destruction.
For the doubting self there is neither this world,
nor the next, nor joy.
Bhagavad Gita 4:39-40

Gospel reading for the day: John 20:19-30
Thomas said, "Unless I see the nail marks in his hands,
and put my finger where the nails were...I will not believe it. "

Third Sunday of Easter

A reading from the Jewish tradition:
"And you are My witnesses, says the Lord, and I am God,"
says the prophet Isaiah. Rabbi Simeon ben Yohai taught,
"If you are 'my witnesses,' I am the Lord, and if you are
not my witnesses, I am not, as it were, the Lord."
Pesikta Kahana 102b

Gospel reading for the day: Luke 24:36-48
"This is what is written: the Christ will suffer and rise from the
dead on the third day.... You are witnesses of these things."

Fourth Sunday of Easter

A reading from the Buddhist scriptures:
"I should be a hostel for all sentient beings,
to let them escape from all painful things.
I should be a protector for all sentient beings,
to let them all be liberated from all afflictions.
I should be a refuge for all sentient beings, to free them
from all fears.... I should accept all sufferings
for the sake of sentient beings, and enable them to escape
from the abyss of immeasurable woes of birth and death....
Why? I would rather take all this suffering on myself
than to allow sentient beings to fall into hell....
I vow to protect all sentient beings and never abandon them.
What I say is true, without falsehood. Why?
Because I have set my mind on enlightenment
in order to liberate all sentient beings;
I do not seek the unexcelled Way for my own sake."
Garland Sutra 23

Gospel reading for the day: John 10:11-18
"I am the good shepherd, who lays down his life for the sheep."

Fifth Sunday of Easter

A reading from the Hindu scriptures:
As the web issues out of the spider
and is withdrawn, as plants sprout from the earth,
as hair grows from the body, even so,
the sages say, this universe springs from
the deathless Self, the source of life.
The deathless Self meditated upon
himself and projected the universe
as evolutionary energy.
From this energy developed life, mind,
the elements, and the world of karma,
which is enchained by cause and effect.
The deathless Self sees all, knows all. From him
springs Brahma, who embodies the process
of evolution into name and form
by which the One appears to be many.
Mundaka Upanishad 1.1.7-9

Gospel reading for the day: John 15:1-8
"I am the vine and you are the branches.
Those who abide in me and I in them bear much fruit,
because apart from me you are nothing."

Sixth Sunday of Easter

A reading from the Buddhist scriptures:
Just as a mother would protect her only child
at the risk of her own life, even so,
cultivate a boundless heart towards all beings.
Let your thoughts of boundless love pervade the whole world.
Sutta Nipata 149-150

Gospel reading for the day: John 15:9-17
"No one has greater love than this,
to lay down one's life for one's friends."

The Ascension of the Lord | Same as Year A

Seventh Sunday of Easter

A reading from the Sikh scriptures:
Yoga consists not in frequenting wild places,
tombs and cremation grounds,
nor in falling into trances;
nor lies it in wandering about the world,
nor in ritual bathing.
To live immaculate amidst the impurities of the world—
this is true Yoga practice.
Adi Granth, Suhi M.1

Gospel reading for the day: John 17:6-19
Jesus prays for his disciples:
"As thou didst send me into the world,
so I have sent them into the world...."

Pentecost

A reading from the Jewish tradition:
Caesar said to Rabbi Gamaliel,
"You state that whenever ten Israelites are assembled,
the Shechinah, the Divine Presence, is found.
How many Shechinahs are there, then?"
Rabbi Gamaliel summoned the ruler's servant,
struck him on the neck, and asked,
"Why did you permit the sun to enter the
house of your master?"
Thereupon the ruler replied,
"The sun shines over all the earth."
Rabbi Gamaliel then said,
"If the sun, which is only one of the
hundred million servants of the Lord,
can shine over all the earth, how much more
would this be true for the Shechinah of the Lord Himself?"
Talmud, Sanhedrin 39a

Gospel reading for the day: John 15:26-16:15
"Unless I go away, the Counselor will not come to you,
but if I go, I will send him to you."

Trinity Sunday
First Sunday after Pentecost

A reading from the Hindu tradition:
The person the pupil gathers the knowledge of his
religious duties from is called the teacher.
The student should never offend the teacher.
For the teacher causes the student to be born
a second time by imparting to him sacred learning.
The second birth is the best;
the father and the mother produce the body only.
Apastamba Dharma Sutra 1.1

Gospel reading for the day: John 3:1-17
Nicodemus came to Jesus under cover of night to talk to him.
"No one can enter the kingdom of God
without being born of water and Spirit."

Sunday between
May 29 & June 4

Use only if after Trinity Sunday

A reading from the Taoist scriptures:
The path into light seems dark.
The way ahead seems to go backwards.
The path into peace seems rough.
The greatest good seems to us empty.
True purity seems stained.
The best efforts seem inadequate.
Appropriate caution seems like cowardice.
True essence seems violated.
The truly square bears no corners.
Sound vessels take time to build.
Celestial music is seldom paid much heed.
The greatest image is impossible to capture.
The Tao is hidden and nameless,
yet it is the Tao alone that nourishes
and completes all things.
Tao Te Ching 41

Gospel reading for the day: Mark 2:23-3:1-6
"The Sabbath was made for man, not man for the Sabbath.
So the Son of Man is Lord even of the Sabbath."

Sunday between June 5 & 11

Use only if after Trinity Sunday

A reading from the Jain scripture:
I have always been solitary; I belong to none else;
I behold no one whom I can say I belong to
nor do I behold one whom I can designate as mine.
The path of worldliness is nothing but disaster.
Who, whose, and where are one's kith and kin?
Who, whose, and where are strangers,
all going round in cycles of birth and death?
At times, the kith and kin become strangers, and vice versa.
Ponder thus, "I am all alone. Nobody was mine in the past,
nor will ever be in the future.
It is because of my karmas that I delude myself
and consider others as mine.
The truth is that I was alone in the past
and will ever be all alone."
Acarangasutra 4:32

Gospel reading for the day: Mark 3:20-35
They said to Jesus, "Your mother and brothers are outside,
asking for you." He replied, "Who are my mother and
my brothers?"

Sunday between
June 12 & 18

Use only if after Trinity Sunday

A reading from the Buddhist scripture:
Do not underestimate good, thinking it will not affect you.
Dripping water can fill a pitcher, drop by drop;
one who is wise is filled with good,
even if one accumulates it little by little.
Dhammapada 9.7

Gospel reading for the day: Mark 4:26-34
The Kingdom of God is like a man scattering
seed on the ground.
When the grain is ripe, he puts it to the sickle,
for the harvest has come.

Sunday between June 19 & 25

Use only if after Trinity Sunday

A reading from the Confucian tradition:
Confucius said,
"The power of spiritual forces in the universe —
how active it is everywhere! Invisible to the eyes
and impalpable to the senses, it is inherent in all things,
and nothing can escape its operation."
It is the fact that there are these forces which make men
in all countries fast and purify themselves,
and with solemnity of dress institute services
of sacrifice and religious worship.
Like the rush of mighty waters,
the presence of unseen Powers is felt;
sometimes above us, sometimes around us.
In the *Book of Songs* it is said,
The hawk soars to the heavens above;
fishes dive to the depths below.
That is to say, there is no place in the
highest heavens above nor in the deepest waters
below where the moral law is not to be found.
Doctrine of the Mean 16, 12

Gospel reading for the day: John Mark 4:35-41
Jesus rebuked the wind and said to the waves, "Quiet! Be still!"
The wind died down and it was completely calm.

Sunday between
June 26 & July 2

A reading from a native American tradition:
Cuts-to-pieces said, "I have a boy of mine,
and he is very sick and
I am afraid he will die soon....
Maybe you can save him for me...."
Everything was ready now, so I made low thunder on the drum,
keeping time as I sent forth a voice. Four times I cried,
"Hey-a-a-hey," drumming as I cried to the Spirit of the World,
and while I was doing this I could feel the power
coming through me from my feet up,
and I knew that I could help the sick little boy.
While I was singing I could feel something queer
all through my body, something that made me want to cry
for all unhappy things, and there were tears on my face....
Then, putting my mouth to the pit of his stomach,
I drew through him the cleansing wind of the north....
Then I told the virgin to help the boy stand up
and to walk around the circle with him,
beginning at the south, the source of life.
He was very poor and weak,
but with the virgin's help he did this.
Next day, Cuts-to-Pieces came and told me that his little boy was
feeling better and was sitting up and could eat something again.
Nicholas Black Elk

Gospel reading for the day: Mark 5:21-43
A woman who suffered from a flow of blood touched Jesus and
was cured. "Daughter, your faith has made you well...."

Sunday between July 3 & 9

A reading from the Islamic scripture:
We gave Abraham of old his proper course,
for We were aware of him, when he said to his
father and his people, "What are these images
to which you pay your devotion?"
They said, "We found our fathers worshippers of them."
He said, "Truly you and your fathers were in plain error....
By God I shall circumvent your idols after you have gone away
and turned your backs." Then he reduced them to fragments,
all save the chief of them....
They said, "Are you the one who has done this
to our gods, Abraham?"
He said, "No, their chief has done it. So question them,
if they can speak." Then they said to Abraham,
"You know well that they do not speak."
He said, "Do you worship instead of God that which cannot
profit you at all, nor harm you? ...Have you no sense?"
They said, "Burn him and stand by your gods, if you will!"
...And we rescued Abraham and Lot, and brought them
to the land that We have blessed for all peoples.
Qur'an 21:51-71

Gospel reading for the day: Mark 6:1-6
"A prophet is not without honor, except in his own country,
and among his own kin, and in his own house."

Sunday between July 10 & 16

A reading from the Buddhist scriptures:
The man whose hands are controlled, whose feet are controlled,
whose words are controlled, who is self-controlled in all things,
who finds the inner joy, whose mind is self-possessed,
who is one and has found perfect peace
—this man I call a monk.
Let him not despise the offerings given to him,
and let him not be jealous of others,
because the monk who feels envy
cannot achieve deep contemplation.
He who wanders without a home in this world,
leaving behind the desires of the world,
and the desires never return—him I call a Brahmin.
He who is free from the bondage of men
and also from the bondage of the gods;
who is free from all things in creation—him I call a Brahmin.
When a mendicant monk, though young,
follows with faith the path of Buddha,
his light shines bright over the world,
like the brightness of a moon free from clouds.
Dhammapada 362, 365, 415, 417, 382

Gospel reading for the day: Mark 6:7-13
Jesus sent them out, two-by-two, and charged them
to take nothing for their journey except a staff;
no bread, no bag, no money in their belts.

Sunday between July 17 & 23

A reading from the Jewish scriptures:
The Lord said to Moses: You yourself are to speak
to the Israelites: "You shall keep my sabbaths,
for this is a sign between me and you throughout
your generations, given in order that you may know
that I, the Lord, sanctify you.... For six days
shall work be done, but the seventh day
is a sabbath of solemn rest, holy to the Lord;
whoever does any work on the sabbath day
shall be put to death. Therefore the Israelites
shall keep the sabbath, observing the sabbath
throughout their generations,
as a perpetual covenant. It is a sign for ever
between me and the people of Israel
that in six days the Lord made heaven and earth,
and on the seventh day he rested,
and was refreshed."
Exodus 31:12-17

Gospel reading for the day: Mark 6:30-34, 53-56
After their missionary journey, Jesus implores
the apostles to rest. But the people will not leave
them alone, and Jesus ministers to them anyway.

Sunday between July 24 & 30

A reading from the Islamic tradition:
A man came to find the Prophet
and asked his wives for something to eat.
"We don't have anything but water," they replied.
"Who wants to share his meal with this
man?" asked the Prophet.
A man of the Companions then said, "I."
Then he led this man to his wife and said to her,
"Treat the guest of God's Messenger with generosity."
She told him, "We don't have anything
but the children's supper."
"Oh, well," he replied, "get the meal ready, light the lamp,
and when the children want supper, put them to bed."
So the woman prepared the meal, lit the lamp,
and put the children to bed. Then, getting up as if to trim the
lamp, she extinguished the flame instead.
The Companion and his wife then made as if to eat,
but in fact they spent the night with empty stomachs.
The next day when the Companion went to find
the Messenger of God, the latter said to him,
"This night God smiled." It was then that God revealed these
words, "and they prefer the others before themselves,
although there be indigence among them."
Adapted from Hadith of Bukhari

Gospel reading for the day: John 6:1-21
"Where shall we buy bread for these people to eat?"
"Here is a boy with five small barley loaves and two small fish,
but how far will they go among so many?"

Sunday between
July 31 & August 6

A reading from the Hindu tradition:
My dark one
stands there as if nothing's
changed,
after taking entire
into his maw
all three worlds
the gods
and the good kings
who hold their lands
as a mother would a child in her womb—
and I by his leave have taken him entire
and I have him in my belly
for keeps.
Nammalvar, Hymns for the Drowning

Gospel reading for the day: John 6:24-35
"The bread of God is he who comes down from heaven
and gives life to the world."
"Sir," they said, "from now on give us this bread."

Sunday between August 7 & 13

A reading from the Sufi tradition:
The drink sent down from Truth,
we drank it, glory be to God.
And we sailed over the Ocean of Power,
glory be to God.
Beyond those hills and oak woods,
beyond those vineyards and gardens,
we passed in health and joy, glory be to God.
We were dry, but we moistened.
We grew wings and became birds.
We married one another and flew,
glory be to God.
…We became servants at Taptuk's door.
Poor Unus, raw and tasteless,
finally got cooked, glory be to God.
Yunus Emre

Gospel reading for the day: John 6:35-51
"I am the bread of life. He who comes to me will never go
hungry, and he who believes in me will never be thirsty."

Sunday between August 14 & 20

A reading from a native European tradition:
I am parched with thirst, and perishing.
But drink of me, the ever-flowing spring on the right,
where there is a fair cypress tree.
Who are you? Where are you from?
I am a child of Earth and of starry Heaven,
but my race is of Heaven alone.
Orphic Lamella from Thessaly

Gospel reading for the day: John 6:51-58
"I am living bread who came down from heaven.
Whoever eats of this bread will live forever...."

Sunday between August 21 & 27

A reading from the Hindu scriptures:
Oh wonderful! I am food!
I am a food eater!
I am a fame-maker!
I am the first-born of the world-order,
earlier than the gods, in the navel of immortality!
Who gives me away, he indeed has aided me!
I, who am food, eat the eater of food!
I have overcome the whole world!
He who knows this, has a brilliantly shining light.
Such is the mystic doctrine.
Taittiriya Upanishad 3.10.5-6

Gospel reading for the day: John 6:55-69
"For my flesh is real food and my blood is real drink.
Whoever eats my flesh and drinks my blood
remains in me, and I in him."

Sunday between
August 28 & September 3

A reading from the Sikh scriptures:
The Brahmin's sacred thread binds not his
passions and lust for woman.
Each morning his face is covered with shame.
By the thread his feet and hands are not restrained;
nor his slanderous tongue and lustful eyes....
Listen, O world! To this marvel:
this man, blind in soul, is called wise.
Adi Granth, Asa-ki-Var M.1

Gospel reading for the day: Mark 7:1-8, 14-15, 21-23
"Listen! What makes a person unclean is not by ingesting
unclean things, but by emitting the evil things in one's heart...."

Sunday between
September 4 & 10

A reading from the Jewish tradition:
I call heaven and earth to witness whether Jew or Gentile,
whether man or woman, whether servant or freeman,
they are all equal in this: that the Holy Spirit rests
upon them in accordance with their deeds!
Seder Eliyyahu Rabbah 10

Gospel reading for the day: Mark 7:24-37
A Phoenician woman begged Jesus to drive the demon
out of her daughter. "First let the children eat all they want,"
he told her, "for it is not right to take the children's bread
and toss it to their dogs."
"Yes, Lord," she replied, "but even the dogs under the table
eat the children's crumbs."

Sunday between September 11 & 17

A reading from the Baha'i scripture:
O Son of Man!
If you love Me, turn away from yourself;
and if you seek My pleasure, regard not your own;
that you may die in Me and I may eternally live in you.
Hidden Words of Baha'u'llah, Arabic 7

Gospel reading for the day: Mark 8:27-38
"Those who want to save their life will lose it, and those
who lose their life for my sake, and for the sake
of the gospel, will save it."

Sunday between
September 18 & 24

A reading from the Taoist scriptures:
To pursue learning is to grow a little more every day.
To pursue the Tao is to desire a little less every day.
Desire less and less,
until you arrive at "not-doing."
When you practice "not-doing," nothing is left undone.
If you want to have the whole world, have nothing.
If you are always busy doing something,
you cannot enjoy the world.
Tao Te Ching 48

Gospel reading for the day: Mark 9:30-37
"If anyone wants to be first, he must be the very last,
and the servant of all."

Sunday between
September 25 & October 1

A reading from the Baha'i tradition:
There can be no doubt that whatever the peoples of the world,
of whatever race or religion, they derive their inspiration
from one heavenly Source, and are the subjects of one God.
The difference between the ordinances under which they abide
should be attributed to the varying requirements
and exigencies of the age in which they were revealed.
All of them, except for a few which are the outcome
of human perversity, were ordained of God,
and are a reflection of His Will and Purpose.
Gleanings from the Writings of Baha'u'llah

Gospel reading for the day: Mark 9:38-50
"Whoever is not against us is for us."

Sunday between October 2 & 8

A reading from the Hindu scriptures:
The husband receives his wife from the gods;
he does not wed her according to his own will.
Doing what is agreeable to the gods,
he must always support her while she is faithful.
"Let mutual fidelity continue until death;"
this may be considered as a summary
of the highest law for husband and wife.
Laws of Manu 9:95, 101

Gospel reading for the day: Mark 10:2-16
"Whoever divorces his wife and marries another
commits adultery against her...."

Sunday between October 9 & 15

A reading from the Confucian scriptures:
The Master said,
"As to being a Divine Sage or even a Good Man,
far be it from me to make any such claim.
As for unwearying effort to learn
and unflagging patience in teaching others,
those are merits that I do not hesitate to claim."
Analects 7:33

Gospel reading for the day: Mark 10:17-30
"Why do you call me good? No one is good but God alone."

Sunday between
October 16 & 22

A reading from the Taoist scriptures:
Know the active, the masculine
yet keep to the passive, the feminine
and you will cradle the world.
If you lovingly hold the world
you will know eternal goodness
and will become again as a little child.
Be aware of the obvious—the light
but keep to the mysterious—the dark
and set an example for the world.
Be an example for the world
and do not stray from your calling
and you will return to the Eternal.
Tao Te Ching 28

Gospel reading for the day: Mark 10:35-45
"Let one of us sit at your right and
the other at your left in your glory."
"You don't know what you are asking....
You know that those who are regarded as rulers of the gentiles
lord it over them.... It shall not be so with you."

Sunday between
October 23 & 29

A reading from the Sikh scriptures:
Under the shelter of the Supreme Being,
not a whiff of hot air touches us—
all around us is drawn the mystic circle of divine protection,
keeping away from suffering.
We have met the holy Preceptor, perfection incarnate,
who has established this state.
He has administered medicine of the divine Name,
and attached our devotion to the Sole Lord.
The divine Preserver has preserved us,
and all maladies removed.
Says Nanak, In His grace has the Lord come to succor us.
Adi Granth, Bilaval M.5

Gospel reading for the day: Mark 10:46-52
A blind man, Bartimaeus, was sitting by the roadside begging.
When he heard that it was Jesus of Nazareth, he began to shout,
"Jesus, Son of David, have mercy on me!"

Sunday between
October 30 & November 5

A reading from the Taoist scriptures:
In the age when life on earth was full,
no one paid any special attention to worthy people....
They were honest and righteous without realizing
that they were "doing their duty."
They loved each other and did not know
that this was "love of neighbor."
They deceived no one yet they did not know
that they were "people to be trusted."
They were reliable and did not know
that this was "good faith."
They lived freely together giving and taking,
and did not know that they were generous.
For this reason their deeds have not been narrated.
They made no history.
Chuang Tzu

Gospel reading for the day: Mark 12:28b-34
"Which commandment is the first of all?"
"...'You shall love the Lord your God with all your heart'...
the second is 'You shall love your neighbor as yourself.'"

All Saints Day

November 1 or First Sunday in November

A reading from the Islamic scripture:
And among his signs is this: you see the earth
barren and desolate, but when We send down rain to it,
it is stirred to life and yields increase.
Truly, He who gives life to the dead earth
can surely give life to men who are dead.
For He has power over all things.
Qur'an 41.39

Gospel reading for the day: John 11:32-43
Jesus called in a loud voice, "Lazarus, come out!"
The dead man came out, his hands and feet wrapped
with strips of linen and a cloth around his face.

Sunday between
November 6 & 12

A reading from the Buddhist scriptures:
Giving is the noble expression
of the benevolence
of the mighty.
Even dust, given in childish innocence,
is a good gift.
No gift that is given in good faith
to a worthy recipient can be called small;
its effect is so great.
Jatakamala 3.23

Gospel reading for the day: Mark 12:38-44
"This poor widow has put in more than all those who are
contributing to the treasury. For they all contributed out
of their abundance, but she out of her poverty...."

Sunday between
November 13 & 19

A reading from the Sekai Kyusei Ko tradition:
Civilization as we know it is only transitory;
it will finally pass away as the new age dawns
and the true civilization is born.
That will mark the end of the "provisional" world
we live in today.... Until now evil forces have had
wide latitude in civilization, but in the transition
from the old to the new, they will be weeded out.
All people will go through an inexorable process of cleansing.
The world will be terribly afflicted in payment for untold sins
gathered over millennia.... In the upheaval, every sphere
of life and every corner of civilization will be transformed.
Those who believe in God and repent will witness the coming
of the new world, and they will be able to start on the
road to salvation. But those still heavily burdened
with sin and unable to overcome their malicious ways
will end this life in absolute misery and may find
no salvation in the next.
Sekai Kyusei Kyo, Johrei

Gospel reading for the day: Mark 13:1-8
"When you hear of wars and rumors of wars, do not
be alarmed; this must take place, the end is still to come....
This is but the beginning of the birth pangs."

Christ the King
Sunday between November 20 & 26

A reading from the Sufi tradition:
So a prophet's soul is especially afflicted,
because it has to become so powerful.
A hide is soaked in tanning liquor and becomes leather.
If the tanner did not rub in the acid,
the hide would get foul-smelling and rotten.
The soul is a newly-skinned hide, bloody and gross.
Work on it with manual discipline,
and the bitter tanning-acid of grief,
and you'll become lovely, and *very* strong.
If you can't do this work yourself, don't worry.
You don't even have to make a decision,
one way or another. The Friend, who knows
a whole lot more than you do, will bring difficulties,
and grief, and sickness, as medicine, as happiness,
as the essence of the moment when you're beaten,
when you hear "checkmate" and can finally say,
with Hallaj's voice, "I trust you to kill me."
Rumi, Mathnawi, IV, 74-109

Gospel reading for the day: John 18:33-37
"It was your own people and your chief priests who
handed you over to me. What is it you have done?"

Thanksgiving Day
Fourth Thursday in November

A reading from the Jewish tradition:
Abraham caused God's name to be mentioned by
all the travelers whom he entertained.
For after they had eaten and drunk,
and when they arose to bless Abraham,
he said to them,
"Is it of mine that you have eaten?
Surely it is of what belongs to God
that you have eaten.
So praise and bless Him by whose word
the world was created."
Talmud, Sota 10b

Gospel reading for the day: Luke 17:11-19
Ten lepers called out, "Jesus, have mercy on us!"
"Go and show yourselves to the priests."
Then one of them turned back, praising God.
"Where are the other nine?" Jesus asked.

Year C

First Sunday of Advent

A reading from a native American tradition:
The holy man told them, "I'll give you something to eat that will kill you, but don't be afraid; I'll bring you back to life again." They believed him. They ate something and died, then found themselves walking in a new, beautiful land. They spoke with their parents and grandparents, and with friends that the white soldiers had killed. Their friends were well, and this new world was like the old one, the one the white man had destroyed. It was full of game, full of antelope and buffalo. All the Indian nations formed one tribe and could understand each other.... Then the holy man brought them back to life. "You have seen it," he said, "the new land I'm bringing. The earth will roll up like a blanket with all that bad white man's stuff, the fences and railroads and mines and telegraph poles, and underneath will be our old-young Indian earth with all our relatives come to life again." Then the holy man taught them a new dance, a new song, a new prayer.... Now everywhere we are dancing this new dance to roll up the earth, to bring back the dead. A new world is coming.

Ghost Dance, Sioux Tradition

Gospel reading for the day: Luke 21:25-36
"Heaven and earth will pass away,
but my words will not pass away."

Second Sunday of Advent

A reading from the Taoist scriptures:
If you don't want to be broken, bend.
If you want to be straight, allow some crookedness.
If you want to be filled, become empty.
If you want to be made new, let yourself be used.
If you want to be rich, desire little.
Wanting more and more is craziness!...
When the ancients said, "If you don't want to be broken, bend,"
Were they just uttering empty words?
Bend sincerely and wholeness will return to you.
Tao Te Ching, 22

Gospel reading for the day: Luke 3:1-6
"Prepare the way for the Lord, make straight paths for him."

Third Sunday of Advent

A reading from the Sufi tradition:
Our laws are different from other laws.
Our religion is like no other.
It is different from the seventy-two sects.
We are guided by different signs, in this world and hereafter.
Without the cleansing of visible waters,
without any movement of hands, feet, or head—we worship.
Whether at the Kaaba, in the mosque, or in ritual prayer,
everyone carries their own disease.
Which labels refer to whom, no one really knows.
Tomorrow it will be clear who abandoned the religion.
Yunus, renew your soul, be remembered as a friend,
know this power. Listen with the ears of love.
Yunus Emre

Gospel reading for the day: Luke 3:7-18
John said, "You brood of vipers! Who warned you to flee from
the coming wrath? Produce fruit in keeping with repentance...."

Fourth Sunday of Advent

A reading from a Gnostic tradition:
For I am the first, and the last, I am the honored one,
and the scorned. I am the whore and the holy one.
I am the wife and the virgin. I am the mother,
the daughter, and every part of both.
I am the barren one who has borne many.
I am she whose wedding is great
and I have no accepted husband.
I am the midwife and the childless one,
the easing of my own labor.
I am the bride and the bridegroom
and my husband is my father.
I am the mother of my father,
the sister of my husband;
my husband is my child.
My offspring are my own birth,
the source of my power,
what happens to me is their wish.
Thunder, Perfect Mind

Gospel reading for the day: Luke 1:39-45
Mary hurried to a town in the hill country where she entered
Zechariah's home and greeted Elizabeth. When Elizabeth heard
Mary's greeting, the baby leaped in her womb.

Christmas | Same as reading for Year A

First Sunday After Christmas

A reading from the Buddhist tradition:
Meanwhile, the King, having noticed that the Bodhisattva
was missing, inquired concerning his absence, asking:
"Where has the young prince gone? I do not see him anywhere."
So a great crowd of people spread out in all directions
to look for the prince. Shortly, one of the King's advisors
caught sight of the Bodhisattva in the shade of the jambu tree,
seated with his legs crossed, deep in meditation.
Lalitavistara Sutra II

Gospel reading for the day: Luke 2:41-52
When they did not find him, they returned to
Jerusalem to search for him. After three days they
found him in the temple, sitting among the teachers,
listening to them and asking them questions. All who heard
him were amazed at his understanding.

Holy Name of Jesus
Same as reading for Year A

New Year's Day
Same as reading for Year A

Second Sunday after Christmas
Same as reading for Year A

Epiphany
Same as reading for Year A

Baptism of the Lord

A reading from the Jewish tradition:
Rabbi Joshua ben Levi met Elijah at the mouth
of the cave of Rabbi Simeon ben Yohai.
He asked Elijah, "When will the Messiah come?"
Elijah replied, "Go and ask him."
"But where is he?" "At the gate of Rome." "And how shall I
recognize him?" "He sits among the wretched who are suffering
from sores; all the others uncover all their wounds,
and then bind them all up again, but he uncovers
and binds up each one separately, for he thinks,
'Lest I should be summoned and be detained.'"
Then Rabbi Joshua found him and said to him,
"Peace be with you, my Master and Rabbi."
The Messiah replied, "Peace be with you, son of Levi."
He said, "When is the Master coming?" He replied, "Today."
Then Rabbi Joshua returned to Elijah, who said,
"What did he say to you?" He replied, "Peace be with you,
son of Levi." Elijah said, "Then he assured to you and your
father a place in the world to come." The rabbi said,
"He spoke falsely to me, for he said he would come
today, and he has not come."
Then Elijah said, "He meant 'Today, if you
hearken to His voice!'"
Talmud, Sanhedrin 98a

Gospel reading for the day: Luke 3:15-22
The people were waiting expectantly and were all wondering
in their hearts if John might possibly be the Christ.
"One more powerful than I will come, the thongs of
whose sandals I am not worthy to untie."

Sunday Between
January 14 & 20

A reading from the Sufi tradition:
This marriage be wine with halvah,
honey dissolving in milk.
This marriage be the leaves and fruit of a date tree.
This marriage be women laughing together for days on end.
This marriage, a sign for us to study.
This marriage, beauty.
This marriage, a moon in a light-blue sky.
This marriage, this silence fully mixed with spirit.
Rumi

Gospel reading for the day: John 2:1-11
A wedding took place at Cana. "They have no more wine."
"Fill the jars with water...."

Sunday between
January 21 & 27

A reading from the Hindu scriptures:
The Self, indeed, is below. It is above. It is behind.
It is before. It is to the south. It is to the north.
The Self, indeed, is all this. Verily, he who sees this,
reflects on this, and understands this delights in the Self,
sports with the Self, rejoices in the Self, revels in the Self.
Even while living in the body he becomes a self-ruler.
He wields unlimited freedom in all the worlds.
But those who think differently from this have others
for their rulers; they live in perishable worlds.
They have no freedom at all in the worlds."
Chandogya Upanishad 7:25:2

Gospel reading for the day: Luke 4:14-21
In the Synagogue, Jesus stood up to read:
"The Spirit of the Lord is upon me...."
He closed the book and announced,
"Today this scripture has been fulfilled in your hearing."

Sunday Between
January 28 and February 3

A reading from the Buddhist scriptures:
In due course the Buddha went to Kapilavastu, and preached the Dharma to his father. He also displayed to him his proficiency in wonderworking power, thereby making him more ready to receive his Dharma. His father was overjoyed by what he heard, folded his hands, and said to him: "Wise and fruitful are your deeds, and you have released me from great suffering. Instead of rejoicing at the gift of the earth, which brings nothing but sorrow, I will now rejoice at having so faithful a son. You were right to go away and give up your prosperous home. It was right of you to have toiled with such great labors. And now it is right of you that you should have compassion on us, your dear relations, who loved you so dearly, and whom you did leave. For the sake of the world in distress you have trodden the path to supreme reality, which could not be found even by those seers of olden times who were gods or kings.... If you have chosen to remain bound up with the things of this world, you could as a universal monarch have protected mankind. Instead, having conquered the great ills of the Samsaric world, you have become a Sage who proclaims the Dharma for the healing of all. Your miraculous powers, your mature intellect, your definite escape from the countless perils of the Samsaric world—these have made you into the sovereign master of the world, even without the insignia of royalty."

Buddhacarita 16

Gospel reading for the day: Luke 4:21-28
"Today this scripture is fulfilled in your hearing."
"Isn't this Joseph's son?" They asked.
"No prophet is accepted in his hometown...." Jesus continued.

Presentation I February 2 I Same as Year A

Sunday Between
February 4 & 10

A reading from the Islamic scripture:
Believers! Shall I point out to you a profitable course
that will save you from a woeful scourge?
Have faith in Allah and His apostle and fight
for His cause with your wealth and your persons.
That would be best for you, if you but knew it.
He will forgive you your sins and admit you
to gardens watered by running streams;
He will lodge you in pleasant mansions in the gardens of Eden.
That is the supreme triumph.
Believers, be Allah's helpers.
When Jesus the son of Mary said to the disciples:
"Who will come with me to the help of Allah?"
they replied: "We are Allah's helpers."
Qur'an 61:10-11, 14

Gospel reading for the day: Luke 5:1-11
They caught such a large number of fish
that their nets began to break.
"From now on you will be fishers of men," Jesus told them.

Sunday Between
February 11 & 17

A reading from the Confucian scriptures:
The five sources of happiness: the first is long life;
the second, riches;
the third, soundness of body and serenity of mind;
the fourth, love of virtue;
the fifth is an end crowning the life.
Of the six extreme evils,
the first is misfortune shortening the life;
the second, sickness;
the third, distress of mind;
the fourth, poverty;
the fifth, wickedness;
the sixth, weakness.
Book of History 5.4.9

Gospel reading for the day: Luke 6:17-26
"Happy are the poor, for yours is the kingdom of God...."

Sunday Between
February 18 & 24

A reading from the Buddhist scriptures:
Hatreds do not ever cease in this world by hating,
but by love; this is an eternal truth....
Overcome anger by love,
overcome evil by good.
Overcome the miser by giving,
overcome the liar by truth.
Dhammapada 1.5 &17.3

Gospel reading for the day: Luke 6:27-38
"Love your enemies, do good to those who hate you,
bless those who curse you, pray for those who abuse you."

Sunday Between
February 25 & 29

A reading from the Confucian scriptures:
Confucius said, "Is it all over?
I still haven't found anyone who can see his faults
and inwardly accuse himself....
As far as exterior culture goes,
I guess I am comparable to others.
When it comes to personal practice of an ideal life,
I have not attained anything."
Analects, 5:27, 7:32

Gospel reading for the day: Luke 6:39-49
"Can a blind person guide a blind person?
Will they not both fall into a pit?"

Transfiguration of the Lord
Last Sunday After Epiphany

A reading from the Hindu scriptures:
Those whose unwisdom is made pure by the wisdom
of their inner Spirit, their wisdom is unto them a sun
and in its radiance they see the Supreme.
Their thoughts on Him and one with Him,
they abide in Him, and He is the end of their journey.
And they reach the land of never-returning,
because their wisdom has made them pure of sin.
With the same evenness of love they behold a priest
who is learned and holy, or a cow, or an elephant, or a dog....
Those whose minds are ever serene win
the victory of life on this earth.
God is pure and ever one, and ever one they are in God.
Bhagavad Gita, 5:16-19

Gospel reading for the day: Luke 9:28-36
Jesus took Peter and John and James up to the mountain to pray.
The appearance of his face changed, and they saw two men,
Moses and Elijah, talking to him.

Ash Wednesday | Same as reading for Year A

First Sunday in Lent

A reading from the Buddhist scriptures:
Then Mara the evil one drew near to him, and said: "Let the
Exalted One exercise governance, let the Blessed One rule."
"Now what, O evil one, do you have in view,
that you speak this way to me?"
"If the Exalted One were to wish the Himalayas,
king of the mountains, to be gold, he might determine it to be so,
and the mountains would become a mass of gold."
The Exalted One responded: "Were the mountains
all of shimmering gold, it would still not be enough
for one man's wants. He that has seen suffering—
how should that man succumb to desires?"
Then Mara the evil one thought: "The Exalted One knows me!
The Blessed One knows me!"
And sad and sorrowful he vanished then and there.
Samyutta Nikaya 4.2.10

Gospel reading for the day: Luke 4:1-13
Jesus was led by the Spirit in the wilderness,
where for forty days he was tempted by the devil.

Second Sunday in Lent

A reading from the Baha'i scriptures:

O kings of Christendom! Heard ye not the saying of Jesus, the Spirit of God, "I go away, and come again unto you"? Wherefore, then, did ye fail, when He did come again unto you in the clouds of heaven, to draw nigh unto Him, that ye might behold His face, and be of them that attained His Presence? In another passage He saith: "When the Spirit of Truth is come, He will guide you into all truth." And yet, behold how, when He did bring the truth, ye refused to turn your faces toward Him, and persisted in disporting yourselves with your pastimes and fancies. Ye welcomed Him not, neither did ye seek His Presence, that ye might hear verses of God from His own mouth, and partake of the manifold wisdom of the Almighty, the All-Glorious, the All-Wise. Ye have, by reason of your failure, hindered the breath of God from being wafted over you, and have withheld from your souls the sweetness of its fragrance. Ye continue roving with delight in the valley of your corrupt desires. Ye, and all ye possess, shall pass away. Ye shall, most certainly, return to God, and shall be called to account for your doings in the presence of Him Who shall gather together the entire creation.

Gleanings from the Writings of Bahá'u'lláh, 246-7

Gospel reading for the day: Luke 13:31-35
"O Jerusalem, Jerusalem, you who kill the prophets
and stone those sent to you, how often I have longed
to gather your children together as a hen gathers her chicks
under her wings, but you were not willing!"

Third Sunday in Lent

A reading from the Jewish scriptures:
Again, though I say to the wicked, "you shall surely die,"
yet if they turn from their sin and do what is lawful and right—
if the wicked restore the pledge, give back what they have taken
by robbery, and walk in the statutes of life,
committing no iniquity—they shall surely live,
they shall not die.
None of the sins that they have committed
shall be remembered against them;
they have done what is lawful and right,
they shall surely live.
Ezekiel 33:14-16

Gospel reading for the day: Luke 13:1-8
Jesus said, "Do you think that these Galileans were
worse sinners than all the other Galileans because
they suffered this way? I tell you no!
But unless you repent, you too will all perish...."

Fourth Sunday in Lent

A reading from the Islamic tradition:
Abu Huraira reported God's Prophet as saying,
"There is none whose deed alone
would entitle him to get into Paradise."
Someone said, "God's Messenger, not even you?"
He replied, "Not even I, but that my Lord wraps me in mercy."
Hadith of Muslim

Gospel reading for the day: Luke 15:1-3, 11b-32
Jesus tells the parable of the prodigal son: "For this your brother
was dead, and is alive; he was lost, and is found."

Fifth Sunday in Lent

A reading from the Buddhist scriptures:
The World-honored One is very rare;
only with difficulty can he be encountered.
Fully endowed with incalculable merits,
he can rescue and preserve all.
The great teacher of gods and men,
he takes pity on the world,
and living beings in the ten directions
all everywhere receive his favors.
Lotus Sutra, 7

Gospel reading for the day: John 12:1-8
Judas is outraged that Mary is "wasting" valuable perfume
on Jesus' feet. "The poor you always have with you,
so leave Mary alone, for you will not always have me."

Maundy Thursday | Palm Sunday
Passion Sunday or Good Friday | Same as Year A

Easter

A reading from the Buddhist scriptures:
The bodhisattva, the great being, having practiced compassion, sympathy, and joy, attaining the stage of the best loved only son.... For example, the father and mother are worried at heart as they see their son ill. Commiseration poisons their heart; the mind cannot part with the illness. So it is with the bodhisattva, the great being.... As he sees beings bound up in the illness of illusion, his heart aches. He is worried as in the case of an only son.... When a father and mother part with their beloved son as the son dies, their hearts so ache that they feel that they themselves should die together with him. The same is the case with the bodhisattva: as he sees a benighted person fall into hell, he himself desires to be born there, too. He thinks, "Perhaps the man, as he experiences the pain, may gain a moment of repentance where I can speak to him of the Law in various ways and enable him to gain a thought of good." For the father and mother of an only son...always think of the son. If he does wrong, they give kindly advice and lead the boy that he does not do evil any more. The same is the case of the bodhisattva: as he sees beings fall into the realms of hell, hungry ghosts and animals, or sees them doing good and evil in the world of man and in heaven, his mind is ever upon them and not apart from them. He may see them doing all evil, yet he does not become angry or punish with evil intent.
Mahaparinirvana Sutra 470-71

Gospel reading for the day: John 20:1-18
Mary Magdalene went to the tomb and found it empty.
"Woman, why are you crying?" "Rabbi!" She exclaimed. "Do not hold on to me, for I have not yet returned to the Father."

Second Sunday of Easter

A reading from a Gnostic tradition:
Now, if you should recall having read
in the Gospel that Elijah appeared—and Moses—
in Jesus' company, do not suppose that
resurrection is an apparition.
It is not an apparition; rather, it is something real.
Instead, one ought to maintain that the world is an apparition,
rather than resurrection—which became possible,
through our lord, the savior, Jesus the kind.
Treatise on Resurrection

Gospel reading for the day: John 20:19-30
Thomas said, "Unless I see the nail marks in his hands
and put my finger where the nails were,
and put my hand into his side, I will not believe it."

Third Sunday of Easter

A reading from the Buddhist scriptures:
All beings should be accommodated and served by me
as attentively as I would show filial respect to my parents,
due respect to my teachers, to elders, and arhats,
up to the Tathagatas, all in equality.
I would be a good physician to the sick,
a guide to those who have wandered from the path,
setting their feet in the right way.
I would be a light to those who wander in darkness.
I would enable the people in poverty to
discover vaults of treasure.
A bodhisattva should thus benefit all beings in equal treatment,
and bestow his loving care on all beings alike.
And why? Because if a bodhisattva serves all beings,
that is equal to serving Buddhas dutifully.
To hold all beings in high esteem,
and render them respectful services,
that is equal to reverencing and serving the Tathagatas.
To make all beings happy, is to please the Tathagatas.
Gandavyuha Sutra, Vows of Samantabhadra

Gospel reading for the day: John 21:1-19
Jesus asked, "Haven't you caught any fish? Throw your
net on the right side of the boat." They were unable to
haul the net in because of the large number of fish. Jesus
cooked the fish for them. When they had eaten, Jesus asked
Peter, "Simon, do you love me?"

Fourth Sunday of Easter

A reading from the Sufi tradition:
When God said, "My hands are yours,"
I saw that I could heal any
creature in this world;
I saw that the divine beauty in each heart
is the root of all time
and space.
I was once a sleeping ocean
and in a dream became
jealous of a
pond.
A penny can be eyed in the street
and a war can break out
over it amongst
the poor.
Until we know that God lives in us
and we can see Him
there,
a great poverty
we suffer.
Rabia

Gospel reading for the day: John 10:22-30
They gathered around him, saying,
"If you are the Christ, tell us plainly."
"I did tell you, but you do not believe. My sheep listen to my
voice; I know them and they follow me."

Fifth Sunday of Easter

A reading from the Confucian tradition:
He set an example for his consort, and also for his brothers,
and so ruled over the family and the state.
In other words, all you have to do is take this very heart here
and apply it to what is over there.
Hence one who extends his bounty can bring peace
to the Four Seas; one who does not cannot bring peace
even to his own family. There is just one thing
in which the Ancients greatly surpassed others,
and that is the way they extended what they did.
Mencius I.A.7

Gospel reading for the day: John 13:31-35
Jesus said, "My children, I will be with you only a little longer.
Where I am going, you cannot come.
I give you a new commandment: love one another."

Sixth Sunday of Easter

A reading from the Hindu tradition:
There was a demon named Harikesha,
devoted to the Brahmins and to dharma.
From his very birth he was a devotee of Shiva.
His father said, "I think you cannot be my son,
or else you are indeed ill-begotten.
For this is not the behavior for families of demons.
You are by your inborn nature cruel-minded, flesh-eating,
destructive. Do not behave in this evil way
—worshipping Brahmins and Shiva—the behavior
ordained by the Creator for demons should not be abandoned;
just as householders should not perform actions appropriate
to the hermitage. Abandon this human nature
with its complicated scale of rites; you must have been born
from a mortal man, to be set on this wrong path.
Among mortals, the appropriate ritual duty arises
according to caste; and I too have ordained your duty
in the proper way."
But Harikesha went to Benares and performed asceticism until
Shiva accepted him as a great yogi, one of his own hosts.
Matsya Purana 180.5-7

Gospel reading for the day: John 14:23-29
If anyone loves me, he will obey my teaching.
My Father will love him, and we will come to him
and make our home with him.

The Ascension of the Lord | Same as Year A

Seventh Sunday of Easter

A reading from the Taoist scriptures:
People of ancient times possessed oneness.
The sky attained oneness and so became clear.
Earth attained oneness and so found peace.
The Spirit attains oneness and so is replenished.
The Valleys attained oneness and so became full.
All things attain oneness and they flourish.
The ancient leaders attained oneness,
and so became examples for all the world.
All of this is achieved by oneness.
Without oneness, the sky would crack, the Earth explode,
the Spirit exhaust, the valley deplete,
leaders would certainly fall, and all life, perish....
Therefore the highest renown is no renown.
We do not want to glitter like jewels.
We do not want to be hard as stone.
Tao Te Ching, 39

Gospel reading for the day: John 17:20-26
"As you, Father, are in me, and I am in you, may they also be in
us, so that the world may believe that you have sent me."

Pentecost

A reading from the Sikh scriptures:
Says Nanak, "The Master is the Lord's image;
The Lord in the Master pervasive—
Brother! Between these lies no difference."
Adi Granth, Asa Chhant M.4

Gospel reading for the day: John 14:8-17 (25-27)
Philip said to Jesus, "Show us the Father."
Jesus said, "Whoever has seen me has seen the Father."

Trinity Sunday
First Sunday after Pentecost

A reading from the Jain scriptures:
The water from the ocean contained in a pot can neither be called an ocean nor non-ocean, but it can be called only part of the ocean. Similarly, a doctrine, though arising from the Absolute Truth, is neither the Truth nor not the Truth.
Vidyanandi, Tattvarhaslokavartika 116

Gospel reading for the day: John 16:12-15
"I still have many things to say to you, but you cannot bear them now. When the Spirit of truth comes, he will guide you into all the truth; for he will not speak on his own, but will speak whatever he hears, and he will declare to you the things that are to come."

Sunday between
May 29 & June 4

Use only if after Trinity Sunday

A reading from a native American tradition:
I saw a man with a black side and a red side,
braids on the black side
and loose hair on the red.
The braids were wrapped around a red cloth,
the sign of danger.
This meant that prayers would contain any danger.
The loose hair was there for sorrow
so that they could wipe their tears
as those who lament in the Sun Dance.
The man wore buckskin leggings, quill work,
and three rows of eagle claws around his neck,
and was carrying a Pipe.
He had the most beautiful outfit I had ever seen.
The man said:
"When you conduct meetings to heal,
I will be there."
Dawson No Horse

Gospel reading for the day: Luke 7:1-10
"I myself am a man of authority, with soldiers under me.
Do not trouble yourself to come to my house.
But only say the word, and my servant will be healed."

Sunday between June 5 & 11

Use only if after Trinity Sunday

A reading from the Islamic scripture:
Say: "Lord, Sovereign of all sovereignty,
You bestow sovereignty on whom You will
and take it away from whom You please;
You exalt whomever You will
and abase whoever You please.
In Your hand lies all that is good;
You have power over all things,
You cause the night to pass into the day,
and the day into the night;
You bring forth the living from the dead
and the dead from the living.
You give without stint to whom You will."
Qur'an 3.25-27

Gospel reading for the day: Luke 7:11-17
A dead person was being carried out
—the only son of his mother.
Jesus told her, "Don't cry." He touched the coffin,
and said, "Young man, I say to you, get up!"

Sunday between June 12 & 18

Use only if after Trinity Sunday

A reading from the Sikh scriptures:
Let us wash the feet of the faithful,
and dedicate our lives to them.
Let us bathe the dust from their feet,
and offer ourselves to them.
Fortunate are they who serve the faithful,
together let us sing praise of the Divine.
The faithful protect us from many dangers,
and we taste the ambrosial nectar by singing Divine praise.
Seeking the shelter of the faithful,
I have come to their portal, says Nanak,
and I have won perfect joy.
Guru Arjan, Sukhmani 15:6

Gospel reading for the day: Luke 7:36-8:3
One of the Pharisees invited Jesus for dinner. When a woman
who lived a sinful life learned that Jesus was there, she stood at
his feet weeping, and wet his feet with her tears. She wiped them
with her hair, kissed them, and poured perfume on them.

Sunday between June 19 & 25

Use only if after Trinity Sunday

A reading from the Hindu scriptures:
The offspring of Prajapati were of two kinds: gods and demons.
Of these the gods were younger and the demons the older.
They were disputing the possession of these worlds.
The gods said, "Well, let us overpower the demons
at the sacrifice with the Udgitha chant."
They said to speech, "Chant for us!"
"Very well," she said. So speech chanted for them the Udgitha.
Whatever delight is in speech, that she chanted for the gods;
whatever she speaks well, that is for herself.
The demons knew: "By this singer they will overpower us."
They attacked her and pierced her with evil.
The evil that makes one speak what is improper, that is that evil.
...The gods said to the Life Breath, "Chant for us!"
"Very well," he said. So the Breath chanted for them.
The demons knew, "By this singer they will overpower us."
They attacked him and wanted to pierce him with evil.
But just as a lump of earth is scattered when it
strikes on a stone, in the same way they were scattered
in all directions and perished.
Therefore the gods increased, and the demons diminished.
He who knows this increases in himself
and his enemies diminish.
Brihadaranyaka Upanishad 1.3.1-7

Gospel reading for the day: Luke 8:26-39
When the demon-possessed man saw Jesus, he cried out and fell
at his feet: "What do you want with me, Jesus, Son of the Most
High God? I beg you, don't torture me!"

Sunday between
June 26 and July 2

A reading from the Confucian scriptures:
The Master said,
"Danger arises when a man feels secure
in his position. Destruction threatens
when a man seeks to preserve his worldly estate.
Confusion develops when a man has put everything in order.
Therefore the superior man does not forget danger in his
security, nor ruin when he is well established,
nor confusion when his affairs are in order.
In this way he gains personal safety
and is able to protect the empire.
In the *I Ching* it is said:
"What if it should fail? What if it should fail?"
In this way he ties it to a cluster of mulberry shoots
and makes success certain.
Great Commentary on the I Ching 2.5.9

Gospel reading for the day: Luke 9:51-62
"Follow me, proclaim the kingdom of God
in which we are going to live."
And yet many have doubts and responsibilities.

Sunday between July 3 and July 9

A reading from the Hindu scripture:
The Kesin, the long-haired sage, bears fire, he bears water
the Kesin upholds earth and heaven,
the Kesin sees all visions of luster,
the Kesin is called the Light.
Sages with the wind for their girdle
wear the soiled yellow robe;
they go along the course of the wind
where the gods have gone before.
"In the ecstasy of Sainthood
we have ascended on the wind,
and only these bodies of ours
are what you mortals ever see."
The Sage flies through mid-air
while he looks at varied forms,
and he is of every deva
a comrade in doing good.
Adapted from the Rig Veda 10.136.1-4

Gospel reading for the day: Luke 10:1-12, 17-20
Jesus sends forth the seventy as lambs in the midst of wolves
to preach the Kingdom of God. "Behold I have given you
authority to tread upon serpents and scorpions, and over
all the power of the enemy; and nothing shall hurt you."

Sunday between July 10 & 16

A reading from the Sikh scriptures:
Ritual purification, though million-fold,
may not purify the mind.
Nor may absorption in trance still it,
however long and continuous.
Possessing worlds multiple quenches not
the rage of avarice and desire.
A thousand million feats of intellect bring not emancipation.
How then to become true to the Creator?
How to demolish the wall of illusion?
Through obedience to His Ordinance and Will.
Says Nanak, This blessing too is pre-ordained.
Adi Granth, Japuji 1, M.1

Gospel reading for the day: Matthew 7:21-29
"Not everyone who says 'Lord, Lord' will enter the Kingdom,
but only those who do the will of my Father."

Sunday between July 17 & 23

A reading from the Buddhist scriptures:
Though he recites many a scriptural text,
but does not act accordingly, that heedless man
is like a cowherd who counts others' cattle.
He has no share in the fruits of the religious life.
Though he can recite few scriptural texts,
but acts in accordance with the teaching,
forsaking lust, hatred, and ignorance,
with right awareness and mind well emancipated,
not clinging to anything here or in the next life,
he shares the fruits of the religious life.
Dhammapada 19-20

Gospel reading for the day: Luke 10:38-42
Martha, who was busy serving, complained that
Mary wasn't helping her. Jesus told her, "Mary has chosen
the good portion, which shall not be taken away from her."

Sunday between July 24 & 30

A reading from a native African tradition:
We are the children of our Maker
and do not fear that he will kill us.
We are the children of God
and do not fear that he will kill.
Sudanese Dinka Prayer

Gospel reading for the day: Luke 11:1-13
"What father among you, if his son asks for a fish,
will instead of a fish give him a serpent;
or if he asks for an egg, will give him a scorpion?"

Sunday between
July 31 and August 6

A reading from the Buddhist tradition:
"These children and riches are mine";
thinking thus the fool is troubled.
Since no one even owns himself,
what is the sense in "my children and riches"?
Verily, it is the law of humanity that though
one accumulates hundreds of thousands of worldly goods,
one still succumbs to the spell of death.
All hoardings will be dispersed,
whatever rises will be cast down,
all meetings must end in separation,
life must finally end in death.
Udanavarga 1:20-22

Gospel reading for the day: Luke 12:13-21
"Fool! This night your soul is required of you;
and the things you have prepared, whose will they be?"

Sunday between August 7 & 13

A reading from the Islamic tradition:
O people! Fear God, and whatever you do,
do it anticipating death. Try to attain everlasting blessing
in return for transitory and perishable wealth,
power, and pleasures of this world.
Be prepared for a fast passage because here
you are destined for a short stay.
Always be ready for death, for you are living under its shadow.
Be wise like people who have heard the message of God
and have taken a warning from it.
Beware that this world is not made for you to live forever,
you will have to change it for hereafter.
God, glory be to Him, has not created you without a purpose
and has not left you without duties, obligations,
and responsibilities....
You must remember to gather from this life
such harvest as will be of use
and help to you in the hereafter.
Nahjul Balagha, Sermon 67

Gospel reading for the day: Luke 12:32-40
"Be dressed ready for service and keep your lamps burning,
like men waiting for their master to return from a
wedding banquet, so that when he comes and knocks
they can immediately open the door for him."

Sunday between August 14 & 20

A reading from the Zoroastrian scriptures:
Yes, there are two fundamental spirits,
twins which are renowned to be in conflict.
In thought and in word, in action, they are two:
the good and the bad. And between these two,
the beneficent have correctly chosen, not the maleficent.
Furthermore, when these two spirits first came together,
they created life and death, and now,
in the end the worst existence shall be for the deceitful
but Heaven for the truthful person.
Of these two spirits, the deceitful one chose
to bring to realization the worst things.
But the very virtuous spirit, who is clothed in the hardest
stones, chose the truth, and so shall mortals who shall satisfy
the Wise Lord continuously with true actions.
Avesta, Yasna 30:3-5

Gospel reading for the day: Luke 12:49-56
"I have come to bring fire on the earth,
and how I wish it were already kindled!"

Sunday between August 21 & 27

A reading from the Sufi tradition:
Rumi speaking to a crowd muses:
"Watch out for those blood suckers from hell
—because they're everywhere.
And the crowd wisely retorts:
"That sounds serious—what do they look like,
any hints; are they usually disguised?"
Rumi again: "Yes, usually, they are awful tricky!"
"How then to detect them?"
Well,
I have noticed
their eyes will narrow and their faces begin to squint
like prunes
if they hear good
poetry.
Rumi

Gospel reading for the day: Luke 13:10-17
On a Sabbath, Jesus saw a woman crippled for eighteen years.
"Woman, you are set free from your infirmity."
The synagogue ruler was indignant.
"You hypocrites!" Jesus answered him, "Don't each of you on the
Sabbath untie his ox or donkey and lead it out to give it water?"

Sunday Between
August 28 & September 3

A reading from the Sikh scriptures:
I have seen hosts of purists and ascetics,
I have visited the homes of yogis and celibates.
Heroes and demons,
practitioners of purity and drinkers of ambrosia,
hosts of saints from countless religions,
I have seen them all.
I have seen religions from all countries,
but I have yet to see followers of the Creator.
Without love for the Almighty, without grace from the Almighty,
all practices are without a grain of worth.
Guru Gobind Singh

Gospel reading for the day: Luke 14:1-14
"Everyone who exalts himself will be humbled,
and he who humbles himself will be exalted."

Sunday between
September 4 & 10

A reading from the Hindu scriptures:
Freedom from the chains of attachments,
even from a selfish attachment to one's children,
wife, or home; an ever-present evenness of mind
in pleasant or unpleasant events; a single oneness of pure love,
of never-straying love for me; retiring to solitary places,
and avoiding the noisy multitudes; a constant yearning
to know the inner Spirit, and a vision of Truth
which gives liberation: this is true wisdom leading to vision.
All against this is ignorance.
Bhagavad Gita 13:8-11

Gospel reading for the day: Luke 14:25-33
"Whoever comes to me and does not hate father and mother,
wife and children, brothers and sisters, yes, and even life itself,
cannot be my disciple."

Sunday between
September 11 & 17

A reading from the interfaith mystical tradition:
I sat one day with a priest who expounded on the
doctrine of hell.
I listened to him for hours, then he asked me
what I thought of all
he said.
And I replied,
That doctrine seems an inhumane cage;
no wonder the smart dogs
ran off.
Kabir

Gospel reading for the day: Luke 15:1-10
"Suppose one of you has a hundred sheep and loses
one of them. Does he not leave the ninety-nine in the
open country and go after the lost sheep until he finds it?"

Sunday between September 18 & 24

A reading from the Hindu tradition:
O my wealth-coveting and foolish soul,
when will you succeed in emancipating yourself
from the desire for wealth? Shame on my foolishness!
I have been your toy!
It is thus that one becomes a slave of others.
No one born on earth did ever attain to the end of desire....
Without doubt, O Desire, your heart is as hard as adamant,
since though affected by a hundred distresses,
you do not break into pieces!
I know you, O Desire, and all those things that are dear to you!
The desire for wealth can never bring happiness.
Mahabharata, Shanti Parva 177

Gospel reading for the day: Luke 16:1-134
"No man can serve two masters. Either he will hate the one and
love the other, or he will be devoted to the one and despise the
other. You cannot serve both God and money."

Sunday between
September 25 & October 1

A reading from the Taoist tradition:

A man named Fan Ki was very wicked, stirring his neighbors to quarrel and sue one another, inciting them to thievery and rape. One day he died suddenly, but came back to life a day later. He called all his relatives to him and said, "I have seen the king of the dark realm, and he said to me, 'Here the dead receive punishments for their evil. The living have no idea what is in store for them. They must endure pain proportional to the violence they have done to their fellow humans.'" His family thought he was feverish and did not believe him. But Yama, the king of Hell, had decided to make an example of him and warn the people from their evil ways. At Yama's command, Fan Ki took a knife and mutilated himself, saying, "This is my punishment for inciting my neighbors to lead evil lives." He put out both of his eyes, saying, "This is my punishment for having looked with anger at my parents, and at the wives and daughters of other men with lust in my heart." He cut off his right hand, saying, "This is my punishment for having killed a great number of animals." He cut open his body and plucked out his heart, saying, "This is my punishment for causing others to die under torture." At last he cut out his tongue to punish himself for lying and slandering. The story of his astonishing act spread far, and people came from miles around to see the unhappy man. For six days he rolled upon the ground in the most horrible agonies and then he died.

Treatise on Response and Retribution, Appended Tables

Gospel reading for the day: Luke 16:19-31
A rich man goes to hell, and begs to be allowed to warn
his brothers. "They have Moses and the Prophets;
let them hear them."

Sunday between October 2 & 8

A reading from the Islamic tradition:
Ibn Mas'ud reported God's Messenger as saying,
"He who has in his heart faith
equal to a single grain of mustard seed
will not enter hell,
and he who has in his heart
as much pride as a grain of mustard seed
will not enter paradise."
Hadith of Muslim

Gospel reading for the day: Luke 17:5-10
"If you have faith as small as a mustard seed,
you can say to this mulberry tree, 'Be uprooted
and planted in the sea,' and it will obey you."

Sunday between
October 9 & 15

A reading from a native African tradition:
One upon whom we bestow kindness
but will not express gratitude,
is worse than a robber
who carries away our belongings.
Yoruba Proverb, Nigeria

Gospel reading for the day: Luke 17:11-19
Jesus healed ten lepers, but only one returned to thank him,
and he was a Samaritan. Jesus asked, "Were not all ten cleansed?
Where are the other nine?"

Sunday between
October 16 & 22

A reading from the Jewish tradition:
Rabbi Akiba, illiterate at forty,
saw one day a stone's perforation
where water fell from a spring,
and having heard people say,
"Waters wear stones," he thought,
"If soft water can bore through a rock,
surely iron-clad Torah should,
by sheer persistence, penetrate a tender mind,"
and he turned to study.
Talmud, Abot de Rabbi Nathan 6

Gospel reading for the day: Luke 18:1-8
"A judge refused a widow her request for justice.
But she kept coming to him. Finally, he said,
'Because this widow keeps bothering me,
I will see that she gets justice, so that she will not wear me out!'"

Sunday Between
October 23 & 29

A reading from the Taoist scriptures:
When enemies are reconciled,
some resentment invariably remains.
How can this be healed?
Therefore the Sage makes good on his half of the deal,
and demands nothing of others.
One who is truly good will keep his promise.
One who is not good will take what he can.
Heaven doesn't choose sides.
It is always with the good people.
Tao Te Ching 79

Gospel reading for the day: Luke 19:1-10
Jesus confronted Zacchaeus, who declared,
"Half of my goods I give to the poor, and if I have
defrauded anyone of anything, I restore it fourfold."
And Jesus said to him, "Today salvation has come
to this house."

Sunday Between
October 30 & November 5

A reading from the Islamic tradition:
The prophet once said,
"Have I not taught you how the inhabitants of Paradise
will be all the humble and the weak,
whose oaths God will accept when they swear to be faithful?
Have I not taught you how the inhabitants of hell
will be all the cruel beings,
strong of body and arrogant?"
Hadith of Bukhari

Gospel reading for the day: Luke 18:9-14
The Pharisee and the tax collector both go to the temple to pray.
Whose prayer did God answer? Jesus said,
"Every one who exalts himself will be humbled,
but he who humbles himself will be exalted."

All Saints Day
November 1 or First Sunday in November

A reading from the Taoist scriptures:
The Sage's heart is not set in stone.
She is as sensitive to the people's feelings as to her own.
She says, "To people who are good, I am good.
And to people who are not good? I am good to them, too."
This is true goodness.
"People who are trustworthy, I trust.
And people who are not trustworthy, I also trust."
This is real trust.
The Sage who leads harmoniously
considers the mind of her people as well as her own.
They look to her anxiously.
They are like her own children.
Tao Te Ching 49

Gospel reading for the day: Luke 6:20-36
"Blessed are you when people hate you and when they exclude
you, revile you, and defame you on account of the Son of Man."

Sunday Between
November 6 & 12

A reading from a native American tradition:
Some day the Great Chief Above will overturn
the mountains and the rocks.
Then the spirits that once lived in the bones buried there
will go back into them.
At present those spirits live in the tops of the mountains,
watching their children on earth and waiting
for the great change which is to come.
The voices of these spirits can be heard
in the mountains at all times.
Mourners who wail for their dead hear spirit voices reply,
and thus they know that their lost ones are always near.
Yakima Tradition

Gospel reading for the day: Luke 20:27-38
"Those who are considered worthy of resurrection
will neither marry nor be given in marriage,
and they can no longer die, for they are like the angels."

Sunday Between
November 13 & 19

A reading from the Islamic tradition:
God's Messenger is reported as saying,
"In the last times men will come forth
who will fraudulently use religion for worldly ends
and wear sheepskins in public to display meekness.
Their tongues will be sweeter than sugar,
but their hearts will be the hearts of wolves.
God will say, 'Are they trying to deceive Me,
or are they acting presumptuously towards Me?
I swear by Myself that I shall send trial
upon those people which will leave the intelligent men
among them confounded.'"
Hadith of Tirmidhi

Gospel reading for the day: Luke 21:5-19
"Watch out that you are not deceived.
For many will come in my name, claiming, 'I am he,'
and, 'the time is near.' Do not follow them."

Christ the King

Sunday Between November 20 & 26

A reading from the Hindu scriptures:
Arjuna said, "And there the sons of Dhritarashtra enter you, all of them, together with a host of kings.... They rush into your awful mouths with those terrible tusks. Some can be seen stuck between your teeth, their heads crushed. As the many river torrents rush toward one sea, those worldly heroes enter your flaming mouths....
I bow before you, supreme God; be gracious. You, who are so awesome to see, tell me, who are you? I want to know you, the very first Lord, for I do not understand what you are doing."
Krishna said, "I am Time who destroys the world of humans. I am the time that is now ripe to gather in the people here; that is what I am doing. Even without you, all these warriors drawn up for battle in opposing ranks will cease to exist. Therefore rise up! Win glory! When you conquer your enemies, your kingship will be fulfilled. Enjoy it. Be just an instrument, you who can draw the bow with the left as well as the right hand!
I myself have slain your enemies long ago.
Do not waver. Conquer the enemies whom
I have already slain....
Fight! You are about to defeat your rivals in war."
Bhagavad Gita 11:26-34

Gospel reading for the day: Luke 23:33-43
They crucified him. Jesus said, "Father, forgive them, for they do not know what they are doing." One criminal said, "Jesus, remember me when you come into your kingdom." Jesus answered him, "Today you will be with me in paradise."

Thanksgiving Day

Fourth Thursday in November

A reading from the Buddhist scriptures:
You, the World Honored One, are a great benefactor.
By doing this rare thing,
you taught us and benefited us
out of your compassion toward us.
No one will be able to repay your favors
even if he tries to do it
for many hundreds of millions of kalpas.
No one will be able to repay your favors
even if he bows to you respectfully,
and offers you his hands or feet or anything else.
No one will be able to repay your favors
even if he carries you on his head or shoulders
and respects you from the bottom of his heart
for as many kalpas
as there are sands in the river Ganges.
Lotus Sutra 4

Gospel reading for the day: John 6:25-35
"It was not Moses who gave you the bread from heaven,
but it is my Father who gives you the true bread from heaven."

Special Days

Presentation

February 2 | Years ABC

A reading from the Buddhist scriptures:
The long-haired sage looked at the baby
and with great joy he picked him up.
Now the Buddha was in the arms
of a man who had waited for him,
a man who could recognize all the signs on his body
—a man who now, filled with delight,
raised his voice to say these words:
"There is nothing to compare with this:
this is the ultimate, this is the perfect man!"
Just then the hermit remembered
that he was going to die quite soon
—and he felt so sad at this that he began to cry.
Sutta-Nipata 689-691

Gospel reading for the day: Luke 2:22-40
Simeon took Jesus up in his arms and praised God, saying,
"Lord, now let your servant depart in peace, for my eyes have
seen the savior which you have prepared for all people."

Annunciation of the Lord | March 25 | Years ABC
Same as Fourth Sunday of Advent, Year B

Visitation of Mary to Elizabeth | May 31 | Years ABC
Same as Fourth Sunday of Advent, Year C

Holy Cross

September 14 | Years ABC

A reading from the Sikh scriptures:
Man's life is a poison-laden ship, tossed into the ocean;
the shore is not visible as it floats in the midst of the waters.
Neither is there oar in hand, nor a pilot in this terrible, vast sea.
Friend! The world is caught in a mighty snare,
only by Divine grace and meditating on the holy Name
may humankind stay afloat.
God is the ship; the holy Word the pilot.
Where there is God's Word, neither wind nor fire, nor waves,
nor any frightful forms have power:
there the holy eternal Name alone abides,
which carries humankind across the ocean of worldliness.
Those going over it, by Divine grace reach the other shore.
Engrossed in devotion to the Eternal,
their transmigration is ended,
their light is merged into the light of the infinite.
Adi Granth, Maru Ahtpadi, M.1

Gospel reading for the day: John 3:13-17
"Just as Moses lifted up the serpent in the wilderness,
so must the Son of Man be lifted up....
Those who believe in me are not condemned."

Sources

Sources are listed by religion, in alphabetical order of the traditional documents cited.

BAHA'I

Kitáb-i-Íqán, Book of Certitude, 152, 176
Sixth Sunday of Easter, A
Bahá'u'lláh (Wilmette, IL: National Spiritual Assembly of the Bahá'ís of the United States, 1931, 1950), p. 152.

Gleanings from the Writings of Baha'u'llah
Sunday between September 25-Oct. I, B
(Wilmette, IL: National Spiritual Assembly of the Bahá'ís of the United States, 1952, 1976), p. 111.

Gleanings...
Second Sunday in Lent, C
pp. 246-7.

BUDDHISM

Anguttara Nikaya, ii.37-39
Sunday between January 14 & 20, B
Buddhists Texts Through the Ages, Edward Conze, ed. (NY: Philosophical. Library, 1954).

Anguttara Nikaya iii:65
Third Sunday of Advent, A
The Kalama Sutta, from *The Life of the Buddha*, Nanamoli Thera (Osbert Moore), trans. (Kandy, Sri Landa: Buddhist Publishing Society, 1972), 175-76.

Buddhacarita
Christmas, ABC
Buddhist Scriptures, Edward Conze, trans. (NY: Penguin Books, 1959), p. 35-36.

Dhammapada 1.5 & 17.3
Sunday between February 18 & 24, C
Dhammapada: The Sayings of Buddha, Thomas Cleary, trans. (NY: Bantam Books, 1994), pp. 8, 77.

Dhammapada 9.7
Sunday between June 12 & 18, B
Cleary, 44.

Dhammapada 19-20
Sunday between July 17 & 23, C
Narada Maha Thera, trans. (Colombo, Sri Lanka: Vajirarama, 1972).

Dhammapada 51-52
Sunday between October 30-Nov. 5, A
Thera.

Dhammapada 362, 365, 415, 417, 382
Sunday between July 10 & 16, B
The Dhammapada, Juan Mascaró, trans. (NY: Penguin Books, 1973).

Digha Nikaya xi.66
Sunday between July 31 & August 6, A
Kevadddha Sutta, *The Lion's Roar: An Anthology of the Buddha's Teachings Selected from the Pali Canon*, David Maurice, ed. (London: Rider & Co., 1962).

Gandavyuha Sutra
Third Sunday of Easter, C
Vows of Samantabhadra, *The Two Buddhist Books in Mahayana* (Hong Kong: Rumford, 1936).

Garland Sutra 23
Easter 4, B
The Flower Ornament Scripture: A Translation of the Avatamsaka Sutra (Boston: Shambhala, 1984-1987).

Jatakamala 3.23
Sunday between November 6 & 12, B
Once the Buddha was a Monkey: Arya Sura's Jatakamala, Peter Khoroche, trans. (Chicago: University of Chicago, 1989), p. 21.

Jtaka 31, 49-51
Epiphany, ABC
The Jataka or Stories of the Buddha's Former Births, H.T. Francis, trans. (London: Pali Text Society, 1895-1907; reprinted 1981).

Lalitavistara Sutra I
First Sunday After Christmas, C
The Lalitavistara Sutra: The Voice of the Buddha: The Beauty of Compassion, Gwendolyn Bays, trans. (Berkeley: Dharma Publishing, 1983), p. 203.

Lotus Sutra 4
Thanksgiving Day, A
The Lotus Sutra, Senchu Murano, trans. (Tokyo: Nichiren Shu Headquarters, 1974).

Lotus Sutra 5
Sunday between July 3 & July 9, A
The Lotus of the Wonderful Law, W. E. Soothill, trans. (Oxford: Oxford University Press, 1930).

Mahaparinirvana Sutra 470-71
Easter, C
Kosho Yamamoto, trans. (Ub e City: Karinbunko, 1973-75; c. Bukkyo Dendo Kyokai).

Mahaparinirvana Sutra 575-76
Sunday between February 11 & 17, B
Yamamoto, trans.

Mahaparinivrvana Sutra 575-76
Sunday between June 26-July 2, B
Yamamoto, trans. Adapted by John Mabry.

Majjhima Nikaya i.101
Second Sunday of Easter, A
Cetokhila Sutta from *Middle Length Sayings* I. B. Horner, trans. (London: Pali Text Society, 1954-59).

Parinirvana
Ascension, ABC
Conze, 62-63.

Samyutta Nikaya 4.2.10
First Sunday in Lent, C
The Book of the Kindred Sayings (Samyutta-Nikaya) or Grouped Suttas: Part I (Kindred Sayings with Verses, Rhys Davids, CAF & Suriyagoda Sumangala Thera, trans. (London: Pali Text Society, 1950), p. 146.

Sutra of Hui Neng 10
Sunday between January 28 & Feb. 3, B
Wong Mou-lam, trans. (Boston: Shambhala, 1969).

Sutta Nipata 149-150
Sixth Sunday of Easter, B
The Sutta-Nipata, H. Saddhatissa, trans. (London: Curson Press, 1985), p. 16.

Sutta-Nipata 689-691
Presentation, ABC
Saddhatissa, p. 80.

Udana 73
Second Sunday after Epiphany, A
Lion's Roar...

Udanavarga 1:20-22
Sunday between July 31 & Aug. 6, C
The Dhammapada with the Udanavarga, Raghavan Iyer, ed. (Santa Barbara, CA: Concord Grove Press, 1986), pp. 235-36.

Vinaya Pitaka i.21
Sunday between June 12 and June 18, A
Some Sayings of the Buddha, F.L. Woodward, trans. (London: Oxford University Press, 1973).

Zen proverb
Maundy Thursday, ABC
World Scripture: A Comparative Anthology of Sacred Texts, Andrew Wilson, ed. (NY: Paragon House, 1991), p. 586.

CONFUCIANISM
Analects, 5:27, 7:32
Sunday Between February 25 & 29, C
The Essential Confucius, Thomas Cleary, trans. (NY: HarperCollins, 1992), p. 117.

Analects of Confucius 7.8
Sunday between January 21 & 27, B
Arthur Waley, trans. (London: George Allen & Unwin; NY: Random House, 1938).

Analects of Confucius 7:33
Sunday between October 9-15, B
Waley.

Book of History 5.4.9
Sunday between February 11 & 17, C
Shu Ching: Book of History, A Modernized Edition of the Translations of James Leggge, Clae Waltham, trans. (Chicago: Henry Regnery, 1971).

Book of History, 5.9
Sunday between July 17 & 23, A
Waltham.

Doctrine of the Mean 16, 12
Sunday between June 19 & 25, B
The Wisdom of Confucius, Lin Yutang, ed. & trans. (NY: Random House, 1938).

Great Commentary on the I Ching 2.5.9
Sunday between June 26 and July 2, C
The I Ching, or Book of Changes, Richard Wilhem, trans. (Princeton: Princeton University Press, 1977).

Mencius I.A.7
Fifth Sunday of Easter, C
Mencius, D. C. Lau, trans. (London: Penguin Books, 1979).

Mencius VI.A.10
Sunday between August 28 and Sept. 3, A
Lau.

GNOSTIC
Thunder, Perfect Mind
Fourth Sunday of Advent, C
The Nag Hammadi Library, James M. Robinson, ed. *(NY: HarperCollins, 1977)*.

Treatise on Resurrection 48:6-16
Second Sunday of Easter, C
The Gnostic Scriptures, Bentley Layton, trans. (NY: Doubleday & Co., 1987).

HINDUISM
Apastamba Dharma Sutra 1.1
Trinity Sunday, B
The Sacred Laws of the Aryas, Sacred Books of the East, vol. 2, George Bühler, trans. (Oxford: Clarnedon Press, 1882).

Bhagavad-Gita 2:28-29
Fifth Sunday in Lent, A
The Bhagavad Gita, Juan Mascaró, trans. (NY: Penguin, 1962).

Baghavad Gita 3:14-16
Easter 5, B
Mascaró.

Baghavad Gita 4:24-25, 28, 30-31
Sunday between August 14-20, B
Mascaró.

Bhagavad Gita 4:39-40
Easter 2, B
The Song of God: Bhagavad-Gita, Swami Prabhavananda adn
Christopher Isherwood, trans. (Hollywood: Vedanta Press, 1944,
1972).

Baghavad Gita, 5: 16-19
Transfiguration of the Lord, C
Mascaró.

Baghavad Gita 8:3-7
Passion Sunday, C
Mascaró.

Bhagavad Gita 11:26-34
Christ the King, C
The Bhagavadgita: A New Translation, Kees W. Bolle, ed. (Berkeley:
University of California Press, 1979).

Baghavad Gita 13:8-11
Sunday between September 4 & 10, C
Mascaró.

Baghavad Gita 17:16-19
Ash Wednesday, ABC
Mascaró.

Brihadaranyaka Upanishad 1.3.1-7
Sunday between June 19 & 25, C
The Vedic Experience: Mantramanjari, Raimundo Panikkar, ed.
(Berkeley: University of California Press, 1977).

Chandogya Upanishad 7:25:2
Sunday between Jan 21-27, C
The Upanishads, Swami Nikhilananda, trans. (NY: Ramakrishna-Vivekananda Center of New York, 1949, 1952, 1956, 1959).

Harivamsa
Fourth Sunday of Advent, A
Hindu Myths, Wendy O'Flaherty, trans. (NY: Penguin, 1975), p. 211.

Isha Upanishad 9-11
Sunday between November 13-19, A
The Upanishads, Eknath Easwaran, trans. (Petaluma, CA: Nilgiri Press, 1985).

Katha Upanishad 2:18-19; Bhagavad Gita, 2:19-20
Easter, ABC
A Dictionary of Religious & Spiritual Quotations, Geoffrey Parrinder, ed. (NY: Simon & Schuster, 1989), p. 194.

Kularnava Tantra 13
Sunday between Sept. 25 & October 1, A
M.P. Pandit (Delhi: Motilal Banarsidass, 1965).

Laws of Manu, 9:95, 101
Sunday between October 2-8, B
The Laws of Manu, Sacred Books of the East, vol. 25, Georg Bühler, trans. (Oxford: Clarnedon Press, 1886).

Matsya Purana 180.5-7
Sixth Sunday of Easter, C
The Origins of Evil in Hindu Mythology, Wendy Doniger O'Flaherty (Berkeley: University of California Press, 1976).

Mahabharata, Shanti Parva 177
Sunday between September 18-24, C
The Mahabharata of Krishna-Dwaipayana Vyasa, Kisarai Mohan
Ganguli, trans. (New Delhi: Munshiram Manoharlal, 1982).

Mundaka Upanishad 1.1.7-9
Fifth Sunday of Easter, A
Easwaran.

Nammalvar
Sunday between July 31-August 6, B
Hymns for the Drowning, A. K. Ramanujan, trans. (Princeton:
Princeton University Press, 1981), p. 67.

Rig Veda 10.9.8-9
Baptism of the Lord, A
Hymns from the Vedas, Abinahs Chandra Bose, ed. (Bombay: Asia
Publishing House, 1966).

Rig Veda 10.136.1-4
Sunday between July 3 & 9, C
Bose; adapted by Mabry.

Shiva Purana
Transfiguration of the Lord, B
Rudrasamhita 18 from *The Shiva Purana* (Delhi: Motilal
Banarsidass, 1970).

Srimad Bhagavatam 1.1
2nd Sunday after Christmas, ABC
Srimad Bhagavatam: The Wisdom of God, Swami Prabhavananda,
ed. (Hollywood: Vedanta Press, 1943).

Taittiriya Upanishad 3.10.5-6, 13
Sunday between August 21 & 27, B
The Thirteen Principle Upanishads, Robert Ernest Hume, trans.
(Delhi: Oxford University Press, 1877), p. 293.

Vishnu Purana 4.24
First Sunday in Advent, B
Adapted from *The Vishnu Purana*, Horace H. Wilson, trans.
(London: John Murray, 1840; London: Trübner, 1864).

ISLAM
Forty Hadith of an-Nawawi 36
Sunday between September 4 and 10, A
An-Nawawi's Forty Hadith, Ezzeddin Ibrahim and Denys
Johnson-Davies, trans. (Damascus: Holy Koran Publishing
House, 1977).

Forty Hadith of an-Nawawi 42
Sunday between September 18 & 24, A
Ibrahim and Johnson-Davies.

Hadith of Bukhari
Sunday between July 24 & 30, B
Muhammad and the Islamic Tradition, Emile Dermenghem, trans.
(trans. from French by J.M. Watt (Westport, CT: Greenwood
Press, 1974).

Hadith of Bukhari
Sunday between October 30 & November 5, C
Dermengham.

Hadith of Muslim
Sunday between October 2 & 8, C
Ahmad.

Hadith of Muslim
Christ the King | November 20-26, A
Ahmad.

Hadith of Muslim
Fourth Sunday in Lent, B
Sahih Muslim, Abdul Hamid Siddiqi, trans. (New Delhi,: Kitab Bhavan, 1977).

Hadith of Muslim
Fourth Sunday in Lent, C
Siddiqi.

Hadith of Tirmidhi
Sunday Between November 13 & 19, C
Mishkat Al-Masabih, James Robson, trans. (Lahore, Pakistan: Sh. Muhammad Ashraf, 1981).

Nahjul Balagha
Sunday between August 7 & 13 , C
Sermon 67, Syed Mohammed Askari Jafery, trns. (Pathergatti, India: Seerat-Uz-Zahra Committee, 1965).

Qur'an 3.27
Sunday between June 5 & 11, C
The Koran, N.J. Dawood, trans. (NY: Penguin, 1956).
Qur'am 4:163-166
Transfiguration, A
Dawood.

Qur'an 14:24-27
Sunday between May 29 and June 4, A
The Koran Interpreted, Arthur J. Arberry, trans. (NY: Macmillan, 1955).

Qur'an 21:51-71
Sundays between July 3-9, B
The Meaning of the Glorious Qur'an, Muhammad Marmaduke
Pickthall, trans. (Mecca and NY: Muslim World League, 1977).

Qur'an 25:63-76
Fourth Sunday After Epiphany, A
Arberry.

Qur'an 41.39
All Saints Day, B
The Meaning of the Glorious Qur'an, A. Yusuf Ali, trans. (Cairo,
Egypt: Dar Al-Kitab Al-Masri, 1938).

Qur'an 61.14
Trinity Sunday I Pentecost 1, A
World Scripture: A Comparative Anthology of Sacred Texts, Maulana
Wahiduddin Khan, trans. (NY: Paragon House, 1991).

Qur'an 61.6
Second Sunday in Advent, B
Ali.

Qur'an 61.10-11, 14
Sunday Between February 4 & 10, C
Dawood.

Qur'an 94
Third Sunday of Easter, A
Arberry.

Sirat Rasul Allah
Fourth Sunday in Advent, B
The Life of Muhammad: A Translation of Ishaq's Sirat Rasul Allah, A Guillaume, trans. (Oxford: Oxford University Press, 1955).

JAIN
Acarangasutra 4:32
Sunday between June 5 & 11, B
Acarangasutra 4:32, from *Acararigasutra*, Muni Mahendra Kumar, trans. (Delhi, Motilal Banarsidass, 1981).

Dr. Sohanlal Gandhi, PhD
Sixth Sunday After Epiphany, A
Dr. Sohanlal Gandhi, PhD in *Pacific Church News*, Autumn 2002, p. 30.

Sutrakritanga
Sunday between August 14 & 20, A
Sutrakritanga 2.1.18-19, from *Jaina Sutras*, Sacred books of the East, vols 22 & 45, Padmanabh S. Jaini, trans. (Oxford: Clarendon Press, 1884 & 1895). ; Wilson 317

Uttaradhyayana Sutra 4:6-7
Sunday between November 6 & 12, A
Jaini. Adapted by Mabry.

Uttaradhyayana Sutra 10.1-4
First Sunday of Advent, A
Jaini.

Vidyanandi, Tattvarhaslokavartika 116
Trinity Sunday, C
Ethical Doctrines in Jainism, K. C. Sogani, trans. (Solapur: Jain Sam. Samraksaka Sangh, 1967).

JUDAISM
Exodus 1-2
1st Sunday after Christmas, ABC
New Revised Standard Version.

Exodus 31:12-17
Sunday between July 17-23, B
New Revised Standard Version.

Ezekiel 33:14-16
Third Sunday in Lent, C
New Revised Standard Version.

Ecclesiasticus 24
Seventh Sunday of Easter, A
New Revised Standard Version.

Hosea 6:1-2
Sunday between February 18 & 24, B
Revised Standard Version.

Isaiah 24: 6-8
Sunday between October 9 & 15, A
New Revised Standard Version.

Pesikta Kahana 102b
Easter 3, B
Hammer on the Rock: A Short Midrash Reader, Nahum N. Glatzer, ed. (NY: Shocken Books, 1948).

Seder Eliyyahu Rabbah 10
Sunday between September 4 & 10, B
Our Masters Taught: Rabbinic Stories and Sayings, Jacob J. Petuchowski (NY: Crossroad, 1982).

Talmud, Abot de Rabbi Nathan 6
Sunday between June 5 and June 11, A
A Rabbinic Anthology, C. G. Montefiore & H. Loewe, eds. (NY: Shocken Books, 1974).

Talmud, Abot de Rabbi Nathan 6
Sunday between October 16-22, C
A Treasurey of Jewish Quotations, Joseph L. Baron, ed. (Northvale, NJ: Jason Aronson, 1985).

Babylonian Talmud, Berakot 5a
Second Sunday in Lent, B
The Babylonian Talmud, I. Epstein, trans. (NY: Soncino Press, 1971).

Talmud, Menahot 29b
Fifth Sunday After Epiphany, A
Ancient Israel: Myths and Legends, Angelo S. Rappoport (Hoboken, NJ: Ktav Publishing House, 1987).

Talmud, Sanhedrin 39a
Pentecost, B
The Talmud for Today, Alexander Feinsilver, trans. Alexander Feinsilver, trans. (NY: St. Martin's Press, 1980).

Talmud, Sanhedrin 98a
Baptism of the Lord, C
Montefiore & Loewe.

Talmud, Shabbat 31a
Sunday between October 23 and 29, A
Epstein.

Talmud, Sota 10b
Thanksgiving Day, A
Montefiore & Loewe.

Talmud, Yoma 86b
Sunday between September 11 and 17, A
Epstein.

Zohar, Genesis 86a
Third Sunday in Advent, B
Baron.

NATIVE TRADITIONS
Native African: Birago Diop, Mali Poem
Easter, B
Muntu: An Outline of the New African Culture, Janheinz Jahn;
Marjorie Grnee, trans. (NY: Grove Press, 1961.

Native African: Dinka Prayer, Sudan
Sunday between October 2 & 8, A
The Prayers of Man: From Primitive Peoples to Present Times,
Alfonso M. di Nola, comp., Patrick O'Connor, ed., Rex Benedict,
trans. (NY: Ivan Obolensky, 1961.

Native African: Fon Song, Benin
New Year, ABC
Au Pays des Fons, Olympe Bhely-Quénum (Paris).

Native African: Igbo Naming Ceremony, Nigeria
First Sunday after Christmas, B
Ofo: Igbo Ritual Symbol, Chirstopher I. Ejizu, adapted by Mabry
(Enugu, Nigeria: Fourth Dimension Publishing Co., 1986).

Native African: Sudanese Dinka Prayer
Sunday between July 24 & 30, C
di Nola.

Native African: Yoruba Proverb, Nigeria
Sunday between October 9-15, C
Yoruba Beliefs and Sacrificial Rites, J.O. Awolalu (London: Longmans, 1979).

Native African: Yoruba song
Fourth Sunday in Lent, A
Yoruba Oral Tradition, Wanda Abimbola.

Native African: Yoruba War Song, Nigeria
Sunday August 14 & 20, C
Abimbola.

Native African: Yoruban War Song
Sunday between June 19 and June 25, A
Abimbola.

Native American: Black Elk
Sundays between June 26 & July 2, B
Black Elk Speaks, Nicholas Black Elk, as told to John G. Neihardt (NY: William Morrow and Co., 1932), pp. 169-171.

Native American: Ghost Dance, Sioux Tradition
First Sunday of Advent, C
American Indian Myths and Legends, Richard Erdoes and Alfonso Ortiz, eds. (NY: Pantheon, 1984).

Native American: Dawson No Horse
Sunday between May 29 & June 4, C
Meditations with Native Americans: Lakota Spirituality, Paul B.
Steinmetz, SJ (Santa Fe: Bear & Co. 1984), p. 63

Native American: George Plenty Wolf
Second Sunday in Lent, A
Steinmetz, p. 57.

Native European: Orphic Lamella from Thessaly
Sunday between August 14 & 20, B
The Ancient Mysteries: A Sourcebook, Marvin Meyer, ed. (NY:
Harper & Row, 1987), p. 101.

Native Middle East: The Birth of Mithra
Holy Name of Jesus, ABC
Payam Nabarz, from her web page dedicated to Mithra
(http://www.bizstore.f9.co.uk/ birth.html).

Neopagan: Wicca chant
Trinity Sunday, A
The Spiral Dance, Starhawk (San Francisco: HarperSanFrancisco,
1979), pp. 183-184.

SHINTO & RELATED MOVEMENTS
Seicho-No-Ie: Nectarean Shower of Holy Doctrines
Lent 5, B
Holy Sutra Nectarean Shower of Holy Doctrines, Masaharu
Taniguchi (Gardena, CA: Seicho-No-Ie Truth of Life Movement,
North American Missionary Hq., 1981).

Sekai Kyusei Ko: Johrei
Sunday between November 13-19, B
Johrei: Divine Light of Salvation (Kyoto: Society of Johrei, 1984).

Moritake Arakida
Palm Sunday, ABC
One Hundred Poems about the World, from *The World of Shinto,*
Norman Havens, trans. (Tokyo: Bukkyo Dendo Kyokai, 1985).

Oracle of Itsukushima
Sunday between June 26 and July 2, A
Readings from World Religions, Selwyn Gurney Champion and
Dorothy Short, comps. (London: Watts & Co., 1951).

SIKH
Adi Granth, Asa-ki-Var, M.1, p. 471
Sunday between August 28 and Sept. 3, B
Sri Guru Granth Sahib, Gurbachan Singh Talib, trans. (Patiala:
Publication Bureau of Punjabi University, Patiala, 1984–).

Adi Granth, Asa Chhant, M.4, p. 442
Pentecost, C
Talib.

Adi Granth, Bilaval, M.5, p. 819
Sunday between October 23-29, B
Talib.

Adi Granth, Gauri, Ravidas, p. 345
Christ the King, B
Talib.

Adi Granth, Gauri Sukhmani, M.5, p. 278
Sunday between February 25 & 29, B
Talib.

Adi Granth, Japuji 1, M.1
Sunday between July 10 & 16, C
Talib.

Adi Granth, Japuji 1, M.1
Sunday between August 7 & 13, A
Talib.

Adi Granth, Maru Ashtpadi, M.1, p. 1009
Holy Cross, ABC
Talib.

Adi Granth, Shalok Sehskriti, M.5, p. 1356
Third Sunday in Lent, B
Selections from the Sacred Writings of the Sikhs, Trilochan Singh et al., trans. (London: George Allen & Unwin, 1960).

Adi Granth, Suhi, M.1, p. 730
Seventh Sunday in Easter, B
Talib.

Adi Granth, Suhi M.5, p. 745
Eighth Sunday after Epiphany, A
Talib.

Adi Granth, Suhi, M.5, p. 745
Sundays between July 10-16, B
Talib.

Adi Granth, Suhi Chhant, M.5, p. 783
Sunday between August 21 and 27, A
Talib.

Adi Granth, Var Majh, M.1, p. 150
Lent 1, B
Talib.

Dhanasri Mahalla 1
Third Sunday After Epiphany, A
The Name of My Beloved, Nikky-Guninder Kaur Singh, trans. (San Francisco: HarperSanFrancisco, 1995), p. 68.

Guru Gobind Singh
Sunday August 28 & September 3, C
Singh, p. 109.

Guru Nanak
Sunday between June 12 & 18, C
Singh, p. 215 #6.

Nikky-Gunider Daur Singh
Baptism of the Lord, B
Adapted by Mabry, from the Introduction to *The Name of My Beloved* by Nikky-Gunider Daur Singh.

SUFI & INTERFAITH MYSTICS
Kabir
Sunday between September 11 & 17, C
Love Poems from God: Twelve Sacred Voices from the East and West, Danel Ladinsky, trans. (NY: Penguin Compass, 2002), p. 215.

Rabia
Fourth Sunday of Easter, C
Ladinsky, 19.

Rumi
Sunday Between January 14 & 20, C
Like This, Coleman Barks with A. J. Arberry, trans. (Athens, GA: Maypop Books, 1990).

Rumi
Christ the King | November 20–26, B
Mathnawi, IV, 74-109, from *We Are Three*, Coleman Barks, trans. (Athens, GA: Maypop Books, 1990), p. 53.

Rumi
Fourth Sunday of Easter, A
We Are Three, p. 67.

Yunus Emre
Sunday between August 7 & 13, B
The Drop that Became the Sea, Kabir Helminski and Refik Algan, trans. (Putney, VT: Threshold Books, 1989), p. 21.

Yunus Emre
Third Sunday of Advent, C
The Drop that Became the Sea, p. 25.

TAOIST
Chuang Tzu 6
All Saints Day, A and
Chuang Tzu: Basic Writings, Burton Watson, trans. (NY: Columbia University Press, 1964).

Chuang Tzu 29
Sunday between October 16 & 22, A
Complete Works of Chuang Tzu, Burton Watson, ed. & trans. (NY: Columbia University Press, 1968).

Chuang Tzu
Sunday between October 30 and Nov. 5, B
The Way of Chuang Tzu, Thomas Merton, trans. (NY: New
Directions, 1965), p. 76.

Tao Te Ching 4
Third Sunday in Lent, A
God As Nature Sees God: A Christian Reading of the Tao Te Ching,
John R. Mabry, trans. (Rockport, MA: Element Books, 1994;
Berkeley, CA: Apocryphile Press, 2004).

Tao Te Ching 22
Second Sunday of Advent, C
Mabry.

Tao Te Ching 28
Sunday between October 16-22, B
Mabry.

Tao Te Ching 29
Sunday between September 11 & 17, B
Mabry.

Tao Te Ching 39
Seventh Sunday of Easter, C
Mabry.

Tao Te Ching 41
Sunday between May 29 & June 4, B
Mabry.

Tao Te Ching 46
Thanksgiving Day, A
Mabry.

Tao Te Ching 48
Sunday between September 18 & 24, B
Mabry.

Tao Te Ching 49
All Saints Day, C
Mabry

Tao Te Ching 63, 73
Seventh Sunday After the Epiphany, A
Mabry.

Tao Te Ching 65
Sunday between July 10 & July 16, A
Mabry.

Tao Te Ching 78
Passion Sunday or Good Friday, A
Mabry.

Tao Te Ching 79
Sunday Between October 23 & 29, C
Mabry.

Treatise on Response and Retribution
Sunday between Sept. 25 and Oct. 1, C
Appended Tables, D.T. Suzuki and Paul Carus, trans. (Peru, IL: Open Court Publishing, 1906, 1973).

ZOROASTRIAN
Avesta, Yasna 30:3-5
Sunday between August 14 & 20, C
The Gathas of Zarathustra, S. Insler, trans. (Leiden: E.J. Brill, 1975).

Avesta, Yasna 30.2-3
Sunday between July 24 & July 30, A
The Hymns of Zarathustra, Jacques Duchesne-Guillemin, M.
Henning, trans. (London: John Murray, 1963).

Avesta, Yasna 45.15
Pentecost, A
Duchesne-Guillemin.

Videvdad 19.1-7
First Sunday in Lent, A
The Zend-Avesta, Part 1: The Vendidad, SAcred Books of the East,
vol. 4, James Darmesteter, trans. (Oxford: Clarendon Press, 1887;
Delhi: Motilal Banarsidass, 1965).

Zend Avesta, Patet 6
Second Sunday of Advent, A
World Scripture, H.K. Mirza, trans.